MANAGING PEOPLE

CIPD REVISION GUIDE 2005

TED JOHNS
IZABELA ROBINSON
JANE WEIGHTMAN

Chartered Institute of Personnel and Development

Published by the Chartered Institute of Personnel and Development,
CIPD House, Camp Road, London, SW19 4UX

First published 2005

Design and typesetting by Curran Publishing Services, Norwich
Printed in Great Britain by The Cromwell Press, Trowbridge, Wiltshire

British Library Cataloguing in Publication Data
A catalogue record of this revision guide is available from the
British Library

ISBN 1 843980 97 5

The views expressed in this revision guide are the authors' own and may
not necessarily reflect those of the CIPD.

The CIPD has made every effort to trace and acknowledge copyright
holders. If any source has been overlooked, CIPD Enterprises would be
pleased to redress this for future editions.

Chartered Institute of Personnel and Development, CIPD House,
Camp Road, London, SW19 4UX
Tel: 020 8971 9000   Fax: 020 8263 3333
Email: cipd@cipd.co.uk   Website: www.cipd.co.uk
Incorporated by Royal Charter. Registered Charity No. 1079797

MANAGING PEOPLE

CIPD REVISION GUIDE 2005

Ted Johns has been a CIPD Chief Examiner for about 20 years and is currently Chief Examiner for both Managing People and People Resourcing. He is an experienced author with a number of publishers.

Izabela Robinson is a Senior Lecturer in Human Resource Management at Northampton Business School. She is a CIPD fellow and spent 10 years as a personnel manager in industry.

Jane Weightman is an honorary lecturer at the Manchester School of Management at UMIST a̶ ... ople textbook.

The Chartered Institute of Personnel and Development is the leading publisher of books and reports for personnel and training professionals, students, and all those concerned with the effective management and development of people at work. For details of all our titles, please contact the publishing department:

tel: 020 8263 3387

fax: 020 8263 3850

e-mail: publish@cipd.co.uk

The catalogue of all CIPD titles can be viewed on the CIPD website:

www.cipd.co.uk/bookstore

CONTENTS

PREFACE

Before settling down to the details of what is required from you as a student attempting the examination in this subject, it is essential to devote some space to clarification of the underpinning philosophy that informs the learning objectives and the indicative content, especially since your assimilation and acceptance of this philosophy is critical to your success.

The objectives and indicative content for Managing People are founded on the belief – itself based on authoritative evidence – that despite the competitive, technological and other pressures applied to UK organisations over recent decades:

- Many employees in many organisations remain massively under-utilised and under developed. Indeed, this is a state of affairs that is frequently admitted (though sometimes subconsciously) in many Managing People examination answers.

- 'In the majority of organisations people are not viewed by top managers as their most important assets' (Guest *et al* 2000). What Guest is saying here is that even when the corporate rhetoric publicises a central concern for people, the organisational reality is far more cynical, mechanistic and manipulative.

- People productivity in the UK economy remains lower than that achieved in many other comparable societies.

Yet nothing can alter the fact that investment with people (like investment with money) can potentially yield a magnificent return in terms of performance, profitability, customer experiences and reputational excellence. As another recent CIPD publication expresses it, 'People management represents the catalytic condition – the essential "X-factor" – that combines other factors into a formula for high performance' (CIPD 2001).

Central to Managing People is the CIPD's strategic vision of people in organisations (whether or not they are employed in the personnel/HR function) as 'thinking performers'. This vision is intended to apply to *all those* who are in some way connected to the performance of an organisation, whatever their level in the hierarchy and whatever their role as a corporate stakeholder (as full-time permanent staff part-time employees, teleworkers, self-employed subcontractors or outsourced agents of some kind). In other words, the obligation to act as a thinking performer is not confined to senior management – even though I fully understand that in today's reality there are many enterprises where the thinking performer vision is little understood and may even be regarded as nothing more than a pious dream.

This understanding was brought home to me very directly when asked an examination question in 2001 about the concept of the thinking performer, long before it had been explicitly articulated in the CIPD's new Professional Development Scheme: I wanted to know what students thought the concept meant, and whether it could work in their own organisations. Although many recognised the point immediately – namely, that people should be constructive and proactive contributors to organisational effectiveness, not merely passive and reactive automatons – there were many others for whom the thinking performer idea presented enormous difficulties:

This vision [of the thinking performer] would not be achievable in my organisation: the senior management are authoritarian and like it that way.

What the senior managers say is not challenged. There is little or no participation or involvement. People are expected to do as they are told. Anyone who has their thoughts on how to do anything keeps these thoughts to themselves. It is very sad and demotivating.

The idea of the thinking performer could only be applied to managers, executives or directors.

It would cost a vast amount of money and waste valuable time [why it would cost so much, and waste time, was not explained, but presumably it was thought that 'thinking' simply diverts attention from 'performing'].

All of the thinking is done at board level [what, none of it at operational level in the personnel/HR function?].

> If applied in my organisation, there would have to be clear guidelines about what was allowed and what was not [so that people would not dare to think about things that were deemed to be nothing to do with them].

> In a production environment, thinking performers would be counter-productive because of the insistence on strict routines, tight procedural controls and close supervision.

What was so depressing about these answers – and they are typical of a significant minority – is that they were produced by putative personnel professionals who eventually, if successful, would become ambassadors for the CIPD. Of course, I acknowledge that many CIPD examination candidates are employed in organisations that do not place their people at the core of their competitive strategy, but it is precisely because of this, and the resultant negative impact on the country's Gross National Product, that the CIPD and the Professional Development Scheme now encapsulate the thinking performer vision – so that we can ultimately break out of the theory X cycle of negative assumptions about people's capabilities, management systems that control and constrain, people who then use their ingenuity to circumvent managerial rules, and managers who then congratulate themselves on the perspicacity of their beliefs about people.

So what does it mean to be a thinking performer? In essence, it involves four separate dimensions:

1. The efficient delivery of expected results and performance of required processes associated with the individual's role and the nature of the organisation – the 'performer' element. People are of little value to an employer unless they do something, but increasingly their ability to do things is not enough – and may not even be the most important dimension of their effectiveness.

2. Periodic reflection on the way processes are currently performed, in order to seek ways of doing them better (to higher standards of cost-effective and customer-relevant quality), cheaper (at lower costs, measured financially or via other means of resource utilisation, including time), or faster (with improved response times and personal/team productivity). Doing what is

done better, faster or cheaper is a key part of continuous improvement – and organisations that do not improve are likely to fall behind competitively to the point where ultimately they go out of business.

3. Challenges about processes, procedures and systems, in order to ensure that these processes, procedures and systems genuinely add value (from the customer's viewpoint) and make a positive difference to organisational outcomes. Even in today's 'lean and mean' organisations, where allegedly costs have been cut to the point where there is no further margin left, it is still possible to find processes, procedures and systems that serve little or no practical purpose other than the provision of false employment opportunities for individuals who could otherwise be doing something that adds genuine value.

4. Clear understanding of and commitment to the purposes behind tasks and activities, so that the 'means' never get in the way of the 'ends'. What I mean by this in everyday language is that properly speaking, people are never employed to undertake tasks, even if that is the impression created in their task-focused job descriptions. In reality, people are employed to achieve results, which may be quite different from performing tasks (indeed, some tasks may actually get in the way of the results). A supermarket checkout operative will undertake a range of activities – passing your goods through the scanner, validating your credit card, and so forth – but these tasks are less important than the ultimate purpose (or mission) associated with the role, which is 'to make the customer want to come back'. If we search for it, every job-holder in every organisation has an ultimate purpose of that kind, which can be energising precisely because it summarises what the job is for, that is, how it (and the job-holder) can add value to the organisation's performance, short-term results and longer-term survival.

In the personnel/HR arena, the thinking performer is the professional practitioner who:

*   consciously seeks to contribute to the underlying strategic vision and goals of the organisation – and therefore understands what they are

- reinforces the compliance role of the personnel/HR function (both legally and ethically), yet fully appreciates that to do so is not a sufficient condition for measuring the effectiveness of the personnel/HR role

- challenges the way things are done in the organisation, the processes, systems and procedures of conventional 'best prac- tice' HRM, in order to search for solutions that are better, cheaper, faster or transformationally different

- keeps in touch with 'customers' through networking in order to understand the business better, react to feedback and construct service innovations that enhance the reputation of the personnel/ HR activity as an added-value contributor.

In case you are still wondering why the thinking performer concept matters, and why it is important for you to be a thinking performer yourself (not simply to enable you to pass the CIPD examinations, but also because the thinking performer paradigm will enhance your own job satisfaction and career prospects), then let me explain further.

Until about 20 years ago, the world of work was (relatively speaking) an uneventful place. Change of all kinds was slow or non-existent; technological innovation, where it occurred at all, was incremental rather than revolutionary; products enjoyed long life cycles; many people had what they believed to be jobs for life, with slow but steady occupational progression; customers were passive and in many instances were compelled to endure products, services and utilities supplied by monopolies; organisations were characterised by central control and universally applied, rule-based systems.

These were the typical features of such organisations in those days (if you read the following list and reflect that your organisation still has many, most or all of these features, then it has to be said that your organisation has not progressed into thinking performer mode):

- hierarchical control through a rigid chain of command, with minimal delegation and jealously guarded authority barriers

- fragmented, directive and mechanistic problem-solving with an emphasis on serial solutions ('What did we do last time?') rather than imaginative, 'off-the-wall' creative thinking and innovation

- single-function specialisms with departmental boundaries, hostile stereotyping and careers concentrated in a single profession (such as 'personnel management'), thus nurturing a narrowness of intellect, self-absorption and a readiness to treat other parts of the same organisation, or even customers, as if they were enemies

- individualism rather than teamwork, reflected in the design of incentive systems and the encouragement of competitive behaviour rather than co-operation

- job descriptions written as lists of tasks and responsibilities, with no reference to 'added value' except, perhaps, at very senior levels

- reactive, procedure-bound systems where performance improvement was almost entirely attributable to the learning/experience curve rather than the deliberate implementation of change.

All these corporate characteristics were exhibited against a background of what I call (in a strange mixture of metaphors), 'slack in the environmental soup': sluggish or non-existent competition, allowing organisations to laze along, carrying superfluous employees (the kind of people known in Japan as 'window watchers' because they have little to do and can therefore gaze out of the window for much of the working day). These employees may have felt comfortable about the fact that they thought they had a job for life, but in practice many were massively under-utilised and under-developed in terms of their potential and their capabilities.

As a case in point, take the television factory at Hirwaun in south Wales. In 1981, run as a joint venture between GEC (now Marconi) and Hitachi, the factory achieved a one-day record output (it was a 'Zero Defect Day' quality campaign) of 1,750 TV sets with 2,200 employees. By 1986, with Hitachi running the business on its own, Hirwaun was routinely churning out 2,400 TV sets, 500 hi-fi units and 500 video recorders every day, with a workforce of only 1,000 employees. Many of these people, moreover, were the same people who had worked there in 1981.

For reasons that need not detain us here, that world has (by and large) gone. It is now fashionable, if not entirely true, to claim that the world of work has become insecure, transient and unreliable;

technological change can cause established products to disappear virtually overnight; product life cycles in some instances can be measured in months rather than years; the 'job for life' seems to have been replaced by a concern for 'employability' and transferable skills; customers have become aggressive, demanding and litigious; erstwhile monopolies now regularly confront competition; globalisation has meant that in the United Kingdom we have continuous access to products and services that have originated in other parts of the world where labour and manufacturing costs are substantially lower; for some skills there is a global labour market and work (especially customer contact activity, many 'back-office' functions and computer software design) can migrate to countries like India; and as a result organisations have to function differently. In a recent article for the *Harvard Business Review*, Kathleen Eisenhardt of Stanford Business School pointed out that 'When the business landscape was simpler, you could afford to have complex plans'; now, by contrast, 'When the environment is so complex, you need a few strategic processes and simple rules to guide people through the chaos' (Eisenhardt and Sull 2001). You need people, in other words, who can think for themselves: thinking performers, no less.

Although the evidence in detail is confusing and ambiguous, there can be no doubting the trends observable from the big picture, namely, the massive transformation in the world of work for most people. (It is likely that you will not have noticed this transformation if you are quite young, because you will have grown up in the midst of the new state of affairs, where the labour market is simultaneously more dangerous and also more exciting.) It is not necessary to be a committed enthusiast for business process re-engineering in order to perceive the relevance and accuracy of some of the predictions advanced by Michael Hammer and James Champy (1993):

- *Work units are changing from functional departments to process teams*: which means more interaction between functions, more cross-departmental communication, more contact with customers, and more attention to the 'process chain' and the extent to which its component parts can justify themselves.

- *Jobs are changing from simple tasks to multi-dimensional work*. In the words of a senior manager at the Rover car manufacturing plant in Longbridge, 'Yes, there has been a massive shift! Fundamentally, we have moved from how a production man would run it to how a businessman would ... that is, it is no longer a question of meeting schedules – we now do that with monotonous regularity.' A similar instance concerns, by coincidence, the Land Rover plant in Solihull, which has undergone a massive culture change since Ford became its new owner. Under previous regimes, the closest workers ever got to driving a Land Rover was helping one to leave the final assembly line, but now they have all been given the chance to drive the cars they make around the company's jungle track. Marin Burela, Land Rover's manufacturing director, has said that 'We've gone from telling people "Come in and build cars" to having a group of people that are thinking' (quoted in the *Daily Telegraph*, 29 May 2001).

- *Roles are changing from 'controlled' to 'empowered'*: In a process team environment, personal development does not always mean climbing up through the hierarchy, but rather constitutes an expansion of breadth, learning more so that one can encompass a larger part of the process. Work then becomes more satisfying, with a greater sense of completion, closure and accomplishment, with greater visibility for outcomes and results, plus more meaning for the individual because of a tangible connection between performance and organisational values. Of course, the corollary is that jobs are more challenging and difficult as the older-style, routine work is eliminated or automated out of existence. Whereas the 'classical' model for organisations comprised what Frederick Winslow Taylor called 'simple jobs for simple people', the new model reflects complex jobs for smart people. (Please don't think this is happening everywhere: there are still plenty of jobs – particularly in call centres where scripted conversations take precedence over customer-related spontaneity – where task disciplines remain tight, but for reasons that are not entirely self-evident.)

- *Values are changing from protection to production*: as employees and organisations begin finally to believe that the ultimate 'boss' is the customer.

- *Managers are changing from supervisors to coaches*: detailed, meticulous control over every aspect of the work process is being replaced by target-setting based on meaningful measures and some degree of process autonomy. Even though many call centres still use 'call duration' as the key measure of employee effectiveness, there are growing numbers that have abandoned that metric on the grounds that it is wholly misleading and may even be counter-productive so far as the customer experience is concerned.

- *Executives are changing from scorekeepers to leaders*: although performance monitoring remains, rightly, an indispensable feature of board-level activity, there is more attention paid to continuous improvement and transformational change through aspirational vision/mission statements and supportive implementation measures.

- *Structures are changing from hierarchical to flat*: and jobs beginning with words like 'deputy' or 'assistant' have all but disappeared. (There is some evidence in favour of a hesitant and tentative return to hierarchy, however, as organisations acknowledge the need to keep each manager's span of control within feasible limits.)

As with everything else, these changes have not occurred everywhere, nor are they universally welcomed across the corporate environment. Until very recently, McDonald's was a hugely successful company, which ran its affairs through highly centralised decision-making, an autocratic management style and minimal amounts of empowerment combined with molecularised job responsibilities. In 1995, responding to a survey in which customers had complained about the impersonality of McDonald's staff, employees were allowed for the first time to select their own words and phrases when greeting and transacting business with customers – but they were still required to secure prior authorisation from their restaurant manager for the words and phrases that they intended to use. Since then, 'empowerment' has gone further as the controlling and centralised reins of the McDonald's business have been progressively relaxed, and they are currently being relaxed even further as the company seeks to recover from what have been its first financial losses for many years. It is certainly arguable that these losses are associated with a culture of centralised decision-making and disenfranchised workers, leading to remoteness from changing customer tastes and some arrogant assumptions about the continued supremacy of McDonald's despite growing competition from more innovative and flexible newcomers.

For most people in the world of work these days – probably including you, and certainly including those who work for McDonald's – the new 'employment charter' embraces these expectations from the employer:

- *We will contract for your services* so long as we believe that your presence in the organisation will add value in some way – by helping our profitability if we are in the private sector, by delivering our services if we are in the public or not-for-profit sectors, by creating customer satisfaction, and by making our corporate survival chances greater in the longer term.

- *You should understand that your job may be in jeopardy* if our circumstances change, and as a result we cannot guarantee you a position for life. If circumstances do arise in which the future relevance of your role becomes questionable, then we may ask you to transfer to fulfil some other, emerging requirement; if that proves impracticable, then we could find ourselves parting company with you. That will be regrettable, but meanwhile we will do our best to ensure that if you do have to leave us, you will nonetheless have some readily transferable skills that will enhance your employability in the labour market.

- *It is not enough simply to perform the basic elements of your job description*, particularly if your job description is drafted in terms of activities and tasks. Instead, you must go out of your way to find opportunities to add value, so that you can genuinely make a difference, becoming a contributor rather than a mere player. Increasingly, we are looking for people who display what is known as 'Organisational Citizenship Behaviour' (OCB), that is, they suggest ideas for beneficial change and process improvement; they help others; they play their full part in team-based activities, cross-functional project groups and so forth; and they are willing to 'go the extra mile' in order to deliver results that advance the organisation's reputation.

- *You must grow and develop alongside the growing and developing requirements of the organisation*. It is necessary to become a 'learning person' just as the organisation becomes a 'learning organisation'. We will provide you with opportunities and encouragement, but ultimately you are your own career-carrier, and for that reason alone, you should be in charge of your own development.

- *You can expect to be rewarded for performance* rather than simply for turning up – and your performance will be measured principally in terms of the added value that you deliver to your customers (whether internal or external). In today's flatter hierarchies, upward career progression in the conventional sense is not likely to be frequent, but there will be considerable chances for lateral moves enabling you to acquire a broad range of competencies that should stand you in good stead as our expectations evolve.

- *Lifetime careers are no longer the norm*. You may want to leave us, or we may want to leave you, typically through no fault of yours. If this does happen, it will be because the 'fit' is no longer right: maybe our needs will have changed in ways which few could have predicted, and even your diligent preparation for an uncertain future will have been misjudged; alternatively, you may have stood still while we have moved on. That in many ways is the most dangerous scenario of all so far as your employability is concerned.

As the phrase 'adding value' or 'added value' has been used several times already, it requires a more detailed explanation, especially as it is inextricably linked to the concept of the thinking performer.

Imagine for a moment that you run your own company, and as part of your expansion programme you think you might recruit me as a full-time customer service manager. You expect to pay me somewhere around £30,000 a year, and on top of that will come all my overheads (office space, pension contributions, National Insurance and so forth), which might amount to another £30,000. So all in all I am going to cost you around £60,000 a year. What do you expect to get for that? Will you be satisfied if I simply 'do a job', as it were, and keep things going, so that customer complaints are handled efficiently, disputes are resolved, and all the necessary administrative support for the customer service department is properly controlled?

Certainly I hope you would want more than that. You might want me to investigate the causes of customer complaints in the hope that the numbers could be reduced or even eliminated altogether; you might want me to build relationships with customers so that our customer retention and customer loyalty levels are increased; you might want me to propose ways in which my function could become a revenue stream (through service contracts, for example) rather than a cost drain. In short, you might want me to add value, to make a difference, to make your organisation better (and more profitable) than it was before. Typically, in fact, you would seek a return on your 'investment' of £60,000 a year, just as you would if you had that kind of money and put it into a building society.

This is the philosophy that permeates the whole of the Managing People learning outcomes and indicative content. In an ideal world (and I would be the first to acknowledge that the real world is far from ideal), people at work are employed because someone thinks their activities will add value. In understanding what this means, it is essential to remember that every job (and I really do mean every job) is a combination of four ingredients:

1. *Maintenance*: fire fighting, or 'keeping the show on the road', or delivering day-to-day operational activities, so that the organisation keeps going. Maintenance does not add value, although not doing it might result in significant loss of value (through industrial accidents, customer defection or discrimination claims by employees who believe they have been treated invidiously).

2. *Crisis prevention*: ensuring that things don't go wrong, that mistakes made in the past are not repeated and that the lessons of experience are properly learned. Crisis prevention does not add value either, although again, failure to do it can cause severe damage to the organisation (if, for example, managerial prejudice against women and/or ethnic minorities is allowed to continue unchecked).

3. *Continuous improvement*: ensuring that what is done is performed to ever-higher standards of quality (as measured by customer reactions), or more quickly, or with fewer demands on

scarce resources. Continuous improvement does add value, even though in some cases its impact only enables the organisation barely to keep up with the growing (and insatiable) demands of customers.

4. *Change management:* generating innovative and different methods, processes and outcomes. Change management definitely adds value, particularly if the organisation is able to gain a competitive advantage as a result of doing something that nobody else has done before.

So, in the personnel/HR arena, for example, 'adding value' is achieved not by process, legal and ethical compliance – these are about maintenance and crisis prevention – but by continuous improvement (better response times, more user-friendly processes) and by change management (new approaches to recruitment and selection, more focused performance management systems and the 'bundling' of people policies into an integrated framework).

'Adding value' is an integral expectation associated with work in many organisations, particularly Japanese companies, those already mentioned in this preface (such as Land Rover) and such world-class enterprises as Singapore Airlines, Shangri-La Hotels, First Direct, the Lands End Clothing Company, Tesco and the RAC. In the Prudential Assurance Company, call centre employees are given a notional budget of £25 per month to 'spend' on creating what Tom Peters calls 'Wow!' experiences for customers. So, when one policy-holder telephoned to ask for a new policy statement for the past year, because her daughter had drawn all over the original, the company sent her a new policy statement – plus a box of crayons and a drawing pad. Result: the customer is hugely impressed and delighted; the reputation and the business success of the company grows as the customer tells others of her treatment; the call centre staff are enthusiastic as well because they are now encouraged to 'think' as well as to 'perform'.

This evidence, admittedly anecdotal, shows why organisations like the Prudential and Land Rover have gone down the 'thinking performer' route. It is certainly not because they are full of the milk of human kindness. They have done it for reasons that are already familiar to those who write about organisations – and that should be equally familiar to those who manage organisations.

The arguments have been eloquently summarised in an article for *People Management* by Robert Kaplan and David Norton (2001):

> A century ago, at the height of the scientific management revolution, companies broke complex manufacturing jobs into sequences of simpler tasks for which industrial engineers and managers set efficient work methods and performance standards. Companies could then hire uneducated, unskilled employees and train them to do a single task.
>
> Today, this mode of work is virtually obsolete. Whatever the organisation – manufacturer or service provider, private or public, for-profit or not-for-profit – all of its employees need to understand and be able to implement its strategy.
>
> The challenge for organisations today is how to enlist the hearts and minds of all their employees. Even those employees involved in direct production and service delivery must strive for continuous improvements in quality, reducing costs and process times to meet customers' expectations and keep up with the competition. ... Doing the job as it was done before is unlikely to be enough.

To write in these terms is to say nothing particularly new. Yet the evidence suggests that even today the majority of employees (at least in the United Kingdom) are systematically mismanaged against the thinking performer paradigm. Thus the Gallup Organisation recently reported on its interviews with a large sample of the UK working population, concluding that there are fundamentally three groups (Buckingham 2001):

1. *The engaged employees*: loyal, productive, task-effective, more inclined to recommend their organisation to friends and family. These constituted a mere 17 per cent of the Gallup sample.

2. *The non-engaged employees*: productive in the sense that they do what is asked of them, yet not psychologically bonded to the organisation and capable of being tempted opportunistically by job vacancies elsewhere; instrumentally motivated, and so responsive to financial incentives but unattracted by higher-order appeals to loyalty. This group made up 63 per cent of the Gallup sample.

3.   *The actively disengaged employees*: physically present but psycho-
     logically absent, characterised by negative, uncooperative atti-
     tudes, hostile behaviour (sometimes in front of customers), and
     a refusal to become involved. These employees formed the
     remaining 20 per cent.

Clearly, what Gallup calls the 'engaged' employees are those who
come nearest to the thinking performer blueprint, and they are
exactly the sort of employees that managers will have in mind when
asked to define the adjective 'good' when used in the phrase 'This
person is good at his/her job'. What managers will typically say is
that someone is a 'good' employee if they achieve the outputs associated with their role, and if they bring some process capabilities to
the performance of their duties. Moreover, there is no shortage of
research – much of it sponsored by the CIPD itself – to show that
'people make the difference'. Summarised below are two examples.

First is the CIPD-funded longitudinal study of 12 organisations,
led by Professor John Purcell, Dr Nick Kinnie and Sue Hutchinson,
all of the School of Management at the University of Bath, published
as *People and performance: unlocking the black box* (Purcell *et al* 2003a),
and outlined in their article for *People Management*, 'Open minded'
(Purcell *et al* 2003b). In explaining what enables some organisations
to deliver superior people performance and commitment, the
authors conclude that good HR policies are not enough. True, good
HR policies can yield 'human capital advantage', which is about
recruiting, developing and retaining good people – but it is easy for
one organisation to copy another in this area, as long as it has the
resources to do so. What makes a bigger difference – and leads to
genuine competitive excellence – is 'organisational process advantage', which reflects the way people work together to be productive
and flexible enough to meet the constant onset of new challenges.
The organisation that achieves a positive combination of 'human
capital advantage' and 'organisational process advantage' will be
unbeatable. In short, 'Human resource advantage can be traced to
better people employed in organisations with better processes'
(Boxall and Purcell 2003, pp85–8).

In this preface there is no space to rehearse the Purcell findings in
detail, but in their six excellent organisations there were two
common and vital ingredients:

1. The excellent organisations all had strong values and an inclusive culture, reflected in a 'big idea', like the pursuit of quality at Jaguar Cars, mutuality at the Nationwide Building Society, and 'living the values' at Tesco.

2. They all had enough line managers who were able to bring HR policies and practices to life in a fashion that recalls the classic combination of 'science' (the systematic policies and practices) plus 'art' (the ability to 'make it happen' with verve and style).

High-performance cultures like these will facilitate 'discretionary behaviour' (or organisational citizenship) through the conscious mobilisation of three 'AMO' ingredients: ability, motivation and opportunity. There must be enough employees with the ability to do what needs to be done; they must think it worthwhile to apply their abilities; and there has to be a positive climate for work-related participation.

The second piece of newly published research is *Sharing the pleasure, sharing the pain*, produced by the European Centre for Customer Strategies in 2003. This investigation has found that in organisations that are truly customer-centric (and whose financial results prove it), customer satisfaction and customer profitability are a daily priority for everyone, not just those who interface directly with external customers or who work in a customer services function. This means that all the enterprise's employees are its ambassadors, and they are therefore 'engaged' (in Gallup's language) as well as being thinking performers (in the CIPD's language).

This preface concludes with some short illustrative examples to demonstrate the fact that the concept of the thinking performer is not some utopian dream, but is a vision that has to be attainable if only because in some organisations it has already been attained.

- Mobil has become a market leader by defining a strategy that enables the company's efforts to be concentrated on key customer segments. This strategy has been assimilated throughout the organisation to such an extent that oil tanker drivers now call in from the field to report problems if they believe that any petrol station is not of a standard to delight the firm's customers.

- Ricardo Semler's new book, *The Seven Day Weekend* (2004) describes how employees at Semco are 'free to question, to analyse, to investigate', and that the company is 'flexible enough to listen'. Just as startling to some audiences is Semler's claim that 'We believe blindly in the virtues of dissent. We don't want a crowd of brainwashed workers. We don't want them to sing company songs, memorise company mission statements and learn to speak only when spoken to ... By letting people off the hook of grand policies, procedures and rules, we release them to be accountable only to themselves.' Powerful stuff – and perhaps all the more impressive when you consider that Semco is a manufacturing business where all too often it is taken for granted that methods have to be rigidly specified and people tightly controlled.

- John Timpson owns the Timpson chain of key-making and shoe repair shops – a decidedly unglamorous business. Because he cannot be everywhere at once, he has to leave his people to get on with it. In retailing this often means adherence to comprehensive rules and procedures, but Timpson has tried a radically different approach. Within limits, employees can charge customers what they like; they can order what stock and supplies they need; they have authority to pay up to £500 to settle complaints. In Timpson's own words, 'We are trying to free people of their inhibitions and enable them to say "Yes" to customers. If customers cannot pay for shoes when they are collecting them, we want our people to be able to say, "Just pay when you come back in." But it's actually difficult to get people to do this. They think I'm mad.' In fact, of course, Timpson is not insane, and the proof is in the figures: for 2002, the company's profitability accelerated by a magnificent 50 per cent.

- The 'Brainwaves' suggestion scheme at the Nationwide Building Society generates savings of around £2 million a year from over 400 implemented ideas. According to John Wrighthouse, the company's head of personnel, the scheme generates cost savings and improved services and products – but it also 'builds loyalty, commitment and a terrific sense of engagement with the Society'. Note the word 'engagement', since it is the same word that Gallup uses to describe those authentically contributing employees.

- In organisations as diverse as the insurance business Direct Line or the manufacturing company Milliken (makers of industrial carpeting and tennis-ball fabric), continuous improvement is built into all role specifications. For Direct Line, indeed, 'continuous improvement' is a core behaviour for all employees, incorporating these six specific actions: seeks ways to improve activities and processes; carries out all activities on the basis of 'getting it right first time'; demonstrates a willingness to try new things and adapt own behaviour; seeks to understand the need for change; demonstrates positive behaviour to requests for change; and proposes ways to comply with requests for change or improvement.

- At Pret A Manger, the fast-food business, would-be new recruits are selected in an interesting and novel fashion. They are required to spend a day working at their nearest Pret A Manger shop – making sandwiches, wrapping them, washing up, clearing tables, the lot – and at the end of the day it is the rest of the team that determines whether they should be accepted into the company or not. In these circumstances, if they are taken on, then the team has a strong obligation to ensure that they are successful, since it was their decision, in effect, to take them on. At Pret A Manger, too, individuals are encouraged to obtain relevant qualifications; when they have done so, they receive an appropriate financial reward, not to keep but rather to share among those in the company who helped them towards success.

- Tesco's culture changes, customer focus and world-class performance feature strongly in the Purcell 'black box' research reports published by the CIPD in 2003. The company has developed its own version of the Kaplan/Norton 'balanced scorecard, now translated into a 'steering wheel' with four quadrants: people, finance, customers, and operations. In the people quadrant, specific targets set for the company and for individual stores include recruitment, development, retention, absence and staff morale. Although the four quadrants are not weighted, one retail director at Tesco, interviewed by Purcell's team, explained that 'If we can recruit, maintain and deliver fantastic people, then operationally we can deliver.' Perhaps surprisingly, given the huge size of Tesco, the people working there demonstrate very high levels of organisational commitment: in the Purcell study, 74 per cent felt proud to tell people who they worked for, 88 per cent felt loyal to Tesco, 86 per cent would recommend a friend or relative to work in Tesco (this is in many ways the crucial acid test, namely, whether you would encourage others close to you to seek employment in the organisation that employs you), and 88 per cent said they shared the values of Tesco.

Out there, in the real world, cultures like these are showing us the way forward. They represent genuinely valuable benchmarking opportunities, particularly as they exemplify the thinking performer concept in action, so you should raise your eyes above your own corporate parapet and seek to learn about the spectacular routes being taken to excellence in the world's leading businesses.

In this way, Managing People entertains worthy ambitions. The Managing People standard is not just about people performance, but focuses equally on excellence – in people's attitudes, commitment, achievements, and contributions.

Based on the work of researchers like Purcell and Jeffrey Pfeffer, we know that the achievement of outstanding excellence depends on the presence of two distinctive elements. First is the presence of a background *infrastructure*, and second, supplementing the infrastructure, is the development and application of *differentiators*.

The *infrastructure* supplies the necessary bedrock without which the organisation cannot attract people at all. It comprises the systems, processes, procedures and ethical/legal compliance ingredients that underpin organisational efficiency. These are what strategists call 'critical failure factors': by themselves, they do not guarantee successful performance, but their absence or neglect will almost certainly guarantee that the employee must suffer reputationally, will be forced to allocate resources to unproductive uses (like defending at employment tribunals), and will be largely populated by employees with instrumental attitudes.

The *differentiators*, on the other hand, are those practices which make the difference – which enable two organisations, ostensibly similar, to produce radically differing results not only in terms of financial outcomes and other significant scorecard measures, but also in terms of people contribution. These are the 'critical success factors', the sources of competitive advantage, the ingredients which turn some employers into 'brands' and 'talent magnets', which stimulate employees to engage in discretionary (organisational citizenship) behaviour – the kind of positive actions that most employers would like their people to display but which they cannot enforce.

This separation between *infrastructure* and *differentiators* is not new. It was signalled in the (then) IPD's position paper, *People make the difference*, in 1994, which pointed out that personnel and development professionals 'need to administer employment systems effectively in compliance with the law and recognised standards of fairness and good practice. *However, that isn't enough. While systems are very important to the smooth running of organisations they don't make the difference between success and failure in the marketplace*' (my emphasis).

Michael Porter's book, *Can Japan compete?* (2000), exposes the fallacy behind the Japanese search for competitive success. In pursuing operational efficiency (that is, *infrastructure* performance) at the expense of seeking genuine *differentiators*, Japanese companies have eventually discovered that 'sooner or later competitors can imitate best practice' and they all end up by running 'unwinnable races down identical paths'.

What this means for people management is that people-management processes and systems are theoretically available to every employer. Once they become established, no employer may gain an advantage in the labour market – or be considered truly 'world-class' – merely by applying these processes and systems.

To get ahead, to attract, retain and motivate people, they must develop some key *differentiators* – perhaps by creating and embedding what Purcell calls the 'big idea', perhaps by selecting primarily for attitude, perhaps by genuine investment in developing people, perhaps by delayering and authentic empowerment, perhaps by people-focused leadership. Plenty of research has been conducted on the 'secrets' of creating what I call a 'contributor culture' to the point where the routes to success are no longer a secret at all. In other words, we now know the difference between those organisations that manage their people systematically, and those organisations that lead their people inspirationally.

Managing People does not adopt a prescriptive, predetermined or formulaic approach to the issue of securing high-performance commitment from people and of generating a 'contributor culture'.

However, it is important to acknowledge that any solutions to this problem must address both *infrastructure efficiency* (the need to do things right) and also *differentiator effectiveness* (the need to do the right things). Moreover, it takes the concept of the thinking performer even further, placing an unequivocal emphasis on the need for evidence-based argument in turn derived from meaningful research into the factors that enable both organisations and individuals to deliver the performance that delights customers, stakeholders, shareholders, investors, employees, HR professionals and society as a whole.

Above all, the examples of organisations like Tesco, Nationwide and the others show what can be done when breaking out of the constraints of processes, systems and compliance – and what therefore we can legitimately expect of you, when you take your CIPD examinations as a thinking performer yourself.

SECTION I

CIPD PROFESSIONAL STANDARDS

I THE CIPD'S MANAGING PEOPLE GENERALIST STANDARD

Summary of standards

The following is based on the standards issued by CIPD for the Professional Standard Managing People. I have directly quoted the standards and mapped material from Jane Weightman's book *Managing people* (2004) which was written to these standards.

The following is a direct quote from the professional standards of the CIPD.

Purpose

It is a truism to claim that while people are a resource, they can (like all resources) be used wastefully, ignored and thrown away, or alternatively harvested fruitfully until they transform themselves from a resource into a capability – a major differentiating strength for the employing organisation.

These standards are about these transformation processes: the people management and leadership practices that can nurture employees who are both able and willing to deliver commitment and performance in today's and tomorrow's employment scenarios. To that end, the standards concentrate less on a spirit of academic detachment in the study of human and organisational behaviour, and focus more on the development of innovative solutions to the issues surrounding the need to maximise people's productivity and effectiveness.

Inspired by the IPD's own 1994 position paper, *People make the difference*, the underpinning philosophy for 'Managing People' is directed towards the preparedness of people to make a positive contribution to the accomplishment of corporate and strategic goals. The goals themselves are founded on the desire for survival, growth and profitability through customer satisfaction and competitive advantage.

It should be noted that although the terms 'leader' and 'leadership' appear periodically within the text for 'Performance Indicators' and 'Indicative content', it is emphatically not expected that individuals undergoing the Core Management standards must subscribe to any 'grand' model of leadership. Within the Managing People module, 'leadership' simply signifies the ability to persuade others (whether colleagues, seniors, suppliers, subordinates or even 'customers') willingly to behave differently from the way they would have acted otherwise. Against this definition, and against the background of typical work patterns in contemporary organizations, 'leadership' is unquestionably a key competence for all aspirant managers and human resource professionals.

Performance Indicators

The full standards include Operational and Knowledge Performance Indicators. These are both given in full here.

Operational Indicators

These 10 Performance Indicators are all examples of demonstrating one's learning at work. By definition they cannot be examined in a written form except as a record of achievement. To indicate the acquisition of the competence or standard you actually need to do something. Mostly this will arise naturally at your place of work. Sometimes you will need to seek out opportunities to practice and demonstrate your competence in these Operational Indicators of performance. There are also exercises that you can do to practice some of the skills. The book *Managing people* by Jane Weightman, which is the accompanying text for this standard, includes activities for you to practise these. These are mapped below against each of the standards.

Practitioners must be able to:

1. Examine their own learning processes analytically in order to apply relevant techniques intended to increase the ability to acquire, retain and apply information, skills and competencies related to personal and organisational effectiveness.

Activities 1–5 in Chapter 3, 'Learning', give some starting points for doing this. By trying to do the activities you will get experience of examining your own learning processes. Not only is this an important skill for managing people it is also very useful when preparing for assessment.

2. Function interpersonally with an enhanced level of self-awareness and with greater sensitivity to the behaviour of others.

Activities 1–7 in Chapter 2, 'Individual differences', ask you to examine your own perceptions. The more we know ourselves and our own particular ways of understanding the more likely we are to be able to understand others and so interact more appropriately.

3. Take account of the 'psychological contract' between organisations and employees, in order to sustain and promote employability within the organisation as well as access the emergent labour market generally.

Activities 1–4 in Chapter 4, 'Factors influencing work, jobs and employment opportunities', give you some opportunities to think about this psychological contract.

4. Actively stimulate and encourage opportunities for the exercise of positive leadership within the organisation.

Activities 1–5 in Chapter 10, 'Leadership', are small ways of practising these skills. By examining the trivial examples in our lives we may become more aware of the nuances of leadership as well as the grand attributes of leadership.

5. Effectively use influence and persuasion skills in the furtherance of corporate goals.

Activities 1–5 in Chapter 11, 'Influence and persuasion', are some starting points for practising influencing and persuasion skills. Again it often the quieter, nudging skills that are more difficult to analyse and develop.

6. Advise on the merits, difficulties and appropriate implementation mechanisms associated with the installation of new and different forms of work pattern and job design aimed at enhancing performance and commitment.

Activities 1–5 in Chapter 5, 'Differing work patterns', give opportunities to practise applying the theoretical models to real examples.

7. Contribute to the implementation of effective performance management processes.

Activities 1–4 in Chapter 14, 'Performance management', give some practical examples to try and a small role-play that may help to develop performance management processes.

8. Plan and implement recruitment/selection systems for identified positions.

Activities 1–6 in Chapter 8, 'Finding and selecting people', ask you to apply the material of the chapter to a real example of recruitment and selection.

9. Contribute to action programmes aimed at resolving problems of poor performance, whether collective or individual.

Figures 28 and 29 in Chapter 14, 'Performance management', would be a beginning. They give some very practical starting points and a sequence to work through when faced with an example of poor performance.

10. Identify training needs and development activities in order to maximise the potential and corporate contribution of others.

Activities 1–5 in Chapter 9, 'Nurturing people', ask you to apply the models and processes given in chapter 9 on training and development to a practical example.

Knowledge Indicators

These 14 Performance Indicators are more easily measured through written examination than the previous group. The CIPD exams are most likely to ask questions about these topics. These Performance Indicators are also more easily written about in textbooks. The relevant sections of Jane Weightman's book *Managing people*, which is the accompanying text for these core standards of the CIPD, are mapped here against the standards.

Practitioners must understand and be able to explain:

1. The principal ways in which human beings differ, the causes of these differences, and the ways in which such differences may be beneficial for both individual and organisational performance.

Chapter 2, 'Individual differences', includes theories of personality such as psychoanalysis, behaviourism and humanistic psychology. It also includes the concepts of perception, diversity and stereotyping.

2. The full range of the linkages between attitudes and behaviour, including recognition of the appropriate initiatives to be exercised in circumstances where the two do not coincide.

Chapter 2, 'Individual differences', looks at whether people's attitudes can be changed. Chapter 14 has material to analyse poor performance, which may help you think about attitudes.

3. The learning process for both individuals and organizations.

Chapter 3, 'Learning', includes behaviourist, experiential and other theories of how people learn. It also has material about Kolb's learning cycle and how different types of learning are appropriate in different situations. The social learning implied in role theory and the 'learning organisation' is examined. Chapter 9, 'Nurturing people', looks at what to train and develop and how to go about it. There is a section on evaluation and lifelong learning.

4. The causes, symptoms, prevention and treatment of (work-related) stress in organizations.

Chapter 6, 'The management of work-related stress', looks at what stress is and the key workplace stressors. Ways of dealing with stress and the role of team leaders are discussed. Specific topics about managing change, time, health and safety are included, with a section on counselling and mentoring.

5. The evolving nature of the 'psychological contract' between organisations and their employees.

Chapter 4, 'Factors influencing work, jobs and employment opportunities', examines the organisational setting. This covers theories of organisational structure and culture. It also looks at the environment in which the organisation operates. Finally, the chapter deals with the employment relationship between organisations and their employees, including the concept of employability.

6. The scenarios in which it may become appropriate for organisations to initiate new types of employment and work patterns, and the mechanisms for organising and implementing such innovations systematically.

Chapter 5, 'Differing work patterns', examines job design, effective work groups, different work patterns and how to manage core and periphery workers.

7. Ethical considerations governing the management and leadership of people.

Chapters 1, 7, 10 and 11 all have material on this issue. Chapter 7 looks at the role of power and control in organisations. Chapter 10 has material on the criteria for effective leadership. Chapter 11 deals with the issue of authority.

8. Methods and techniques for coping with power and conflict in an organisational setting.

Chapter 7, 'The move from compliance to commitment', has political theories about control and participation. Understanding the basis of power in organisations and how conflict is part of organisation life are examined. Empowerment and valuing are also part of understanding the influence of power within organisations.

9. The acquisition, practice and development of leadership skills for the furtherance of corporate/organisational purposes and the difference between 'management' and 'leadership'.

Chapter 10, 'Leadership', has material on leadership traits, roles of leaders, styles of leaders and contingency theories of leadership. The drive for leadership rather than management in organisations is also discussed.

10. Practical frameworks for the exercise of influence and persuasion skills (especially for those lacking any significant degree of hierarchical/legitimised authority).

Chapter 11, 'Influence and persuasion', examines the concepts of authority, credibility, delegation, networking and negotiating. There is practical material on meetings and presentations.

11. The major theories of motivation and their application through job design, reward/recognition systems and performance management.

Chapter 12, 'Motivation', looks at theories of motivation, for example, Maslow and Herzberg, and how motivation is influential at work. Chapter 5 studies job design, while performance management and rewards are dealt with in Chapters 13 and 14.

12. Systematic techniques for dealing with problems of poor performance.

Chapter 14, 'Performance management', ends with systematic approaches of establishing a gap in performance, why there is a gap and then solutions to the reasons.

13. The elements of the recruitment and selection process, with special reference to the production of job descriptions and/or accountability profiles.

Chapter 8, 'Finding and selecting people', looks at systematic ways of identifying vacancies, recruitment methods and different ways of carrying out the selection process.

14. The basic ingredients essential to the effective design and operation of performance review and appraisal systems.

The first half of Chapter 14 describes the process of measuring performance and some of the issues that need to be considered. There is also material about appraisal systems.

Indicative content

The following is a direct quote from the standards. It forms the basis of what a person achieving this professional standard would be expected to know about. This indicative content was the basis of the material included in Jane Weightman's book *Managing people*. Specific chapter references are given above against the Performance Indicators. You might want to check through this list to check that you have covered the whole standard. These are the basis of the content on which you will be examined. You should know what these words mean and have something appropriate to say about them.

1.   *The fundamental characteristics of people*

Individual differences:

- ability and disability
- culture
- background
- gender
- ethnicity
- personality.

Attitudes and behaviour:

- causes, manifestations and implications
- economic, psychological and cultural influences
- linkages (or lack of them) between attitudes and behaviour.

Learning:

- how people learn
- the conditions appropriate to effective learning for both knowledge and skills/competencies.

2.   *The changing world of work*

The psychological contract of employment:

- factors influencing the nature of work and jobs

- 'added-value' performance expectations
- the concept of employability.

People competencies for the newly emergent work roles

- 'customer' focus and corporate orientation
- interpersonal effectiveness through leadership and persuasion rather than legitimised authority.

New work patterns:

- features, benefits and difficulties
- effective implementation and review.

The management of (work-related) stress in organisations:

- causes
- symptoms
- alleviation through prevention and 'treatment'.

3. *Optimising the people contribution*

Overview: the drive for leadership in organisations:

- from 'management' to 'leadership': factors prompting the move from 'compliance' to 'commitment'
- the 'control/participation' dilemma: conflict, power, and the problems of securing acceptance for a partnership culture in organisations
- Finding, selecting and nurturing people fitted for the needs of today and tomorrow's organisations.

Mobilising commitment through effective leadership:

- the visionary and ethical constituents of leadership
- criteria for effective leadership behaviour
- leadership influence and persuasion in action: the practical application of leadership skills in workplace settings.

rough effective motivation:

> y and its actual/potential relevance for 'live'
> orporate scenarios

improved performance through recognition and

- coaching purposes, processes and applications

- the systematic approach to rectifying poor performance

- an overview of performance management: the holistic route for integrating strategy, target-setting, incentives, rewards, appraisal and focused employee behaviour

- training and development needs diagnosis, processes and systems, relating individual competencies to organisational goals/purposes.

Below is the contents table of the book *Managing people* (Weightman 2004). You can see that it follows very closely the indicative content of the standards.

Part 1 The fundamental characteristics of people
1   Introduction to managing people
    Introduction
    What are the different strands of thought that inform this area?
    Central debates about managing people
    How to use this book
2   Individual differences
    Why people have different personalities
    Perception
    Equal opportunities and diversity
    Overcoming stereotyping and prejudice
    Can people's attitude at work be changed?
3   Learning
    How people learn?
    What about individual differences?
    Effective learning in different situations
    Role theory

Keywords

The following list is of the words that you should understand to achieve the Managing People standards. This list can be a useful checklist immediately before exams. The terms are all referred to in Jane Weightman's book *Managing people* (2004) and are referenced in the index of that book so you can quickly look them up. One way of using this keywords list is to try to put definitions by each word – if you do not know one, look it up in a suitable textbook. A normal dictionary is not really precise enough for your needs. Definitions are deliberately not given here as you need to define them yourself to meet the standards for this professional qualification.

Alienation	Employment environment
Appraisal	Empowerment
Assessment	Equal opportunities
Attitudes	Ethics
Authority	Evaluation
Behaviour modification	Experiential learning
Behaviourism	Goals
Career management	Group theory
Classical conditioning	HR
Communication	HR planning
Competencies	Humanistic psychology
Contingency	Initiation
Continuous improvement in	Intelligence
organisations	Interviewing
Control/participation dilemma	Job design
Core competencies	Leaders' behaviours
Counselling	Leaders' roles
Credibility	Leaders' styles
Customers	Leaders' traits
Delegation	Leadership
Development	Learning chain
Discipline	Learning organisations
Dismissal	Learning styles
Diversity	Lifelong learning
Effective teams	Management
Employability	Management by objectives

Managing change
Managing time
Meetings
Mentoring
Morale
Motivation
Networking
Norm
Operant conditioning
Organisational culture
Organisational structures
Organisations' aims
Perception
Performance appraisal
Performance management
Performance-related pay
Periphery staff
Personal constructs
Planning
Pluralist
Political theory

Politics
Poor performer
Power theories
Prejudice
Presentations
Psychoanalysis
Psychological contract
Psychology
Recruitment
Role
Selection
Socialisation
Sociology
Stress
Team
Theories of personality
Training
Unitarist
Valuing
Work patterns

SECTION 2

REVISION AND EXAMINATION GUIDANCE

2 REVISION AND EXAMINATION GUIDANCE

Introduction: The '2 + 10 + 5 + M' formula for success

If you have read the 'thinking performer' part of this revision guide (and if you have not, please do so now: it is in the preface), you will be generally aware of the evaluation criteria that will be applied to your examination script, and indeed to all your scripts for subjects that are listed under the umbrella of the CIPD's Professional Development Scheme. These criteria collectively comprise the '2 + 10 + 5 + M' formula, summarised below.

The Two

These are the CIPD's vision of the personnel/HR professional as a 'business partner' (contributing to the achievement and furtherance of the organisation's broader strategic goals and objectives, and therefore not motivated solely by an insular, isolationist 'professional' imperative) and as a 'thinking performer' – able to deliver day-to-day results but also capable of constructing personal/functional/corporate improvement and change contributions.

The Ten

These are the 10 competencies, which help translate the thinking performer model into plausible, credible behaviour patterns. They are listed in the PDS literature, but are: personal drive and effectiveness; people management and leadership; business understanding; professional and ethical behaviour; added-value result achievement; continuing learning; analytical and intuitive/creative behaviour; 'customer' focus; strategic thinking; communication, persuasion and interpersonal skills.

The Five

The five 'BACKUP' competencies are especially crucial in the context of the PDS examinations, and so here they are outlined in somewhat greater detail:

- *Business orientation* is a focus on results, acceptance of the CIPD vision of personnel/HR practitioners (at all levels) as a business partner and adherence to the view that people are (or should be) employed as 'contributors' in order to add value to their organisation's strategic purposes. A business orientation, moreover, implies a concern for the efficient and effective husbandry and deployment of the organisation's resources, including its people: so employee benefits can only be justified if their advantages (encouraging the retention of talented people) outweigh their costs.

- *Application capability* is the willingness to address practical issues in a decisive, assertive and confident fashion, to develop solutions to problems, to design implementation and action programmes that can translate higher purposes (or a 'big idea') into meaningful outcomes. If a question in the examination calls for recommendations, application capability is present when the recommendations are logically derived from convincing situational analysis, when they are a persuasive mixture of the systematic and the innovative, and when they are presented with sufficient detail to enable them to go beyond the platitudinous.

- *Knowledge of the subject* suggests a thorough grasp of the indicative content, familiarity with the major concepts applicable to the field, and awareness of current/recent developments even if they have not specifically appeared in the syllabus. Given the structure of the Managing People examination these days and the potentially wide range of its Section B coverage, question spotting is virtually impossible and candidates must therefore ensure that their knowledge of the subject is very comprehensive.

- *Understanding* is reflected in the ability to go beyond the mere repetition of fashionable mantras (about, say, emotional intelligence, job enrichment and performance management) and simplistic generalisations (about the 'fact' that happy workers lead to happy customers), but to recognise the ambiguities, subtleties and political complexities of organisational life, and to acknowledge that virtually all beneficial change involves some corresponding trade-offs. Understanding is demonstrated by students when, in their examination scripts, they begin to challenge some of the conventional wisdom about, say, motivation and leadership at work, and particularly when they are able to do so while citing relevant literature sources, benchmarking experience or research findings.

- *Persuasion and presentation skills* implies that scripts are well received when answers are organised systematically, lucidly, cogently and attractively.

All five of these competencies are equally important, and it has to be emphasised that superior performance in one sphere may not be traded off against inferior achievement in another. In effect, there is considerable overlap between all four elements in the '2 + 10 + 5 + M' formula, and so for all practical purposes it is the five 'BACKUP' competencies that should be viewed as crucial.

The 'M'

It is also necessary for you to take note of the fact that Managing People, and the CIPD's Core Programme as a whole, are classified as postgraduate in status – hence the use of the abbreviation 'M', which means 'Master's degree level'. This being so, the following expectations are appropriate as well as all those listed above:

- You must show a systematic understanding of the knowledge linked to the subject matter, and a critical awareness of current problems and/or new insights.

- You must have a comprehensive understanding of Managing People in practice – both in your own organisation and in others.

- You should be equipped with a conceptual understanding that enables you to evaluate critically both current research and methodologies.

In practical terms, this means that any statements of 'fact' produced in your answers must be reinforced by citations from appropriate third-party sources, including research and textbook literature. Possession of a thinking performer attitude and perspective is more important than straightforward knowledge – so, at the margin between pass and fail, what may swing the balance in your favour will be answer material that exemplifies the thinking performer values and demonstrates a broad, strategic perspective, and this will count for more than the extent of your detailed knowledge and your ability therefore to reproduce 'facts'. Equally, factual errors in your script – provided they are infrequent – may be overlooked as long as your approach to the subject is philosophically appropriate.

How to fail

It may seem depressing to list the typical reasons why some candidates fail the examination, and why some continue to do so when re-attempting it a second or third time. Yet it is essential, because these are the 'symptoms' of an inability (or reluctance) to meet the CIPD's professional standards that you must guard against in every aspect of your endeavours – whether reading a textbook, collecting information, practising your examination techniques, or fulfilling your specific accountabilities at work. So let me summarise the most frequently encountered causes for failure, but let me also emphasise at the same time that only one of them will guarantee that you fail. None of the rest will make the essential difference on its own; it is only if they are combined together that the cumulative impact can be, for you, crucially damaging.

You will certainly fail if:

- You do not attempt seven questions in Section B (irrespective of the mark you obtain for Section B as a whole, the mark you secure for Section A, and the mark you accumulate for Section A and Section B added together).

You are likely to fail if you demonstrate one or more of the following:

- Answers that contain no references whatsoever to authoritative, convincing third-party 'evidence' culled from relevant research, literature or textbooks. If your answers do not incorporate material drawn from persuasive sources, the examiners will be entitled to conclude that you have undertaken no systematic preparation or reading for the examination. Moreover, you cannot escape from this obligation to generate evidence-based argument merely by peppering your answers with general phrases like 'Research evidence suggests ...', 'Recent research indicates ...', or, worst of all, 'Research proves ...'.

- Answers that are written from the narrow perspective of a single organisation in a single sector. You have to absorb the principle that the CIPD professional qualification is intended to prepare you to be able to perform competently across a comprehensive range of organisations and a variety of business/economic sectors, so you must demonstrate some well-informed familiarity with people-management practices and contingent considerations over the field as a whole. Armed with such familiarity, you may well then be in a position to avoid the use of uninformed stereotyping about people management in sectors other than the one in which you currently work – so that, for instance, you do not make naïve and unjustified assumptions about the 'evil' effects of the profit motive in the private sector if you happen to work in the public sector, and you do not assume high levels of parasitical activity in the public sector if you happen to work for a profit-seeking enterprise.

- Answers that are long on description and short on critical, analytical evaluation of the kind which is crucial to an 'M'-level discipline, or which write about life in any given organisation as if the employees were selflessly devoted to its corporate purposes, as if everyone worked together in an entirely disinterested manner, and as if systems were designed and then implemented without any difficulties whatsoever. In a recent report I defined this as the 'hagiolatry tendency', where 'hagiolatry' refers (in my dictionary) to 'worship and veneration of the saints'. Here is an example (taken from one of the entries for the May 2004 diet) – the platitudes have been highlighted for ease of interpretation:

> Many high-performing organisations ... may also be called **learning organisations** as they encourage **continuous**

improvement to the organisation, which links directly to continuously improving staff performance by means of **knowledge sharing, continuous training** and **greater communication** throughout the organisation, this in turn makes employees feel **empowered** and contributes towards their **motivation** and **innovation of ideas** which is encouraged.

So, in this sentence of approximately 60 words, about one-third of the content consists of unsubstantiated clichés. What makes it worse is that the candidate was actually seeking to describe Marks & Spencer, which at the time of the May 2004 examination was still struggling to cope with declining profits, declining sales and declining morale.

Preparing for the examination

First, to take this subject seriously, you must buy some textbooks, starting with Jane Weightman's CIPD publication on *Managing people*, whose most recent edition, published in 2004, has been specifically designed around the Managing People standard. This needs to be supplemented, however, with two more specialised sources on the key themes of motivation and leadership that form such a central part of the learning objectives and indicative content for Managing People. These two sources are *The motivation handbook* by Sarah Hollyforde and Steve Whiddett (2002) and *Leadership skills for boosting performance* by Terry Gillen (2002); as an alternative to the latter you could try *Leadership skills* by John Adair (1998). The total cost of these key volumes will be about £57, which may seem a lot of money but it will be well spent as an investment in your own personal learning – as well as being critical to your examination performance.

Second, you must now allocate some time to reading your chosen books, since the knowledge they contain will not transmit itself into your brain merely as a result of owning them. In a disciplined way, allocate a minimum of three one-hour 'active reading' sessions each week throughout your study programme. Select key chapters from the three books (one per 'active reading' session), find a quiet location, remove all distractions, wear earplugs if necessary, sit at a desk or at a table (not in a comfortable armchair, since that only encourages laziness), and start to read, concentrating single-mindedly on the words on each page. The reason why these 'active reading' sessions should not last longer than one hour is that it is very difficult to sustain high levels of focus for more than about 60 minutes (as you will have found when trying to pay attention during a lecture), but if you give yourself fully to the material then your hour will enable a good deal of information to enter your head and stay there. In addition, do everything you can to assist your concentration: take notes, highlight key points, underline quotations and so forth – even read aloud, if it helps.

Third, even though you now have well-informed ideas coming at you from three respected textbooks, you still need to keep up to date as well, because you may find the occasional question in the examination about topics that have become 'hot' issues but were not envisaged when the Managing People Indicative Content was put together, or when the textbooks were written. So, you must study *People Management* every fortnight, and take cuttings from anything that looks potentially useful, especially articles about named organisations and book reviews; you should regularly consult the CIPD website on the Internet and take advantage of the opportunities to gain access to linked sites where useful and up-to-the-minute information can be found. Of course, you should also keep your ears and eyes open in your own organisation, and secure copies of relevant documents like competency frameworks, people strategies and so forth.

If you are working with others as part of your study programme, by attending a college or university, then set up a collaborative group to which everyone contributes, say, one useful document each week – if there is a member who reads the *Daily Telegraph*, or gets it at home, ask them to photocopy any relevant articles from each Thursday's business supplement; if someone admits to seeing the *Financial Times* at their place of work, ask them to scan each issue for articles and features on topics related to people management, so that you can all share the material. It is important to recognise, when embarking on such co-operative ventures, that passing the Managing People examination is not a competitive exercise: the CIPD does not establish a predetermined pass rate and then ensure it is not exceeded; on the contrary, success is available to everyone who satisfies the professional standards. So, theoretically, everyone could pass – as long as they fulfilled the professional standards – and as a result if you collaborate with others, then you have everything to gain: your own study workload is reduced, and your chances of success are enhanced.

Given the emphasis on learning about 'world class' people-management practices, and given the possibility that your own employer may not be 'world class' in that sense, then you should go out of your way to learn about such benchmark enterprises as (in the private sector) Tesco, Nationwide, BMW and the RAC and (in the public sector), Liverpool Council, Fife Council, Westminster City Council and some of the other local authorities classified as 'excellent' in the Government's Comprehensive Performance Assessment (CPA) review, plus other public-sector agencies that have deservedly acquired enviable reputations for customer orientation and focus. You can learn about these organisations (and please note that those named above are not meant to constitute a comprehensive list; they are merely examples) through a number of routes:

- via the CIPD website and in particular the *People Management* archive

- through reading recent CIPD research reports which feature in-depth studies of such organisations, for example, *Bringing policies to life: the vital role of front line managers in people management* by Sue Hutchinson and John Purcell (2003), which deals at length with, among others, Tesco and Selfridges

- Internet searches

- scrutiny of the corporate websites operated by these organisations themselves.

Keep all your cuttings, your photocopies, your original documents and your items downloaded from the Internet, and then purchase a cardboard concertina file (about £5), and label the compartments with the titles of each of the major sections from the indicative content. Going through these materials just prior to the examination must form a major ingredient in your revision planning – again, taking notes, underlining key points, highlighting quotations, even reading aloud, in order to maximise the learning and retention potential from the exercise.

Fourth, you need to practise your examination techniques to ensure that you are fully prepared for the examination itself. This involves a number of distinct steps:

- Set yourself the goal of attaining a mark of at least 60 per cent, so that you have a safety margin in case, on the day, you don't perform at your best or the balance of questions is unattractive to you. It is very dangerous to rely on simply 'satisficing', or doing just enough work to get by with a mark of 50 per cent: many have failed the examination in this way, because it is a high-risk strategy. By contrast, if you go into the examination fully expecting to achieve a mark of 60 per cent, your self-confidence will be boosted and, in fact, your actual performance will be even better.

- Look at past question papers, not in an effort to 'spot' favoured topics (that is virtually impossible, given the structure of the paper), but to tease out the character of the examination and the likely expectations associated with the chief examiner's approach.

- Assess yourself initially along, say, a 10-point scale (zero being low, 10 being high), against the five 'BACKUP' competencies: business orientation, application capability, knowledge of the subject matter, understanding, and persuasion/presentation skills. Then create a personal development plan focusing on those competencies that most need to be developed: your plan should involve a combination of reading, practice, tutor feedback and further practice.

- Attempt some typical past questions, from both sections of the paper. Initially you do not need to stick rigorously to examination conditions, but produce your answers with the aid of every form of assistance you can find, such as the textbook, your concertina-file papers, and guidance from your tutor or from someone well informed in your own organisation.

- When you have completed some answers, leave what you have written for 24 hours and look at your answers again, this time trying to do so from the perspective of the chief examiner. Ask yourself how your answer could have been improved; write down the improvements; evaluate your material once more.

- Then seek some expert feedback from your tutor or from a suitable mentor, asking him or her to take note of the 'BACKUP' formula and to structure the advice around its five dimensions.

- Undoubtedly you should also develop your examination technique under properly simulated conditions, especially to ensure that you can adhere to the appropriate time-management rules. You should not spend more than an hour on Section A, and you must then devote the second hour to Section B (and in that time you have to respond to seven questions from a possible 10). In general, the chief examiner believes it is preferable to tackle Section A first, since that is the part that requires most preparatory thought – and that is how you can profitably spend the initial 10 minutes of thinking time before the examination proper begins. Obviously, you may prefer to apportion your time differently – many successful candidates attempt part of Section B first, and then Section A, then return to Section B, but what you must do is find time to do everything that is required of you.

- In your answers, remember that you have to impress the examiners with your command of the five 'BACKUP' competencies. The examiners will not know that you have read some textbooks or some *People Management* articles, or some features in the *Financial Times*, unless you specifically tell them: so, if you have some third-party sources that you can acknowledge, then you must do so. Equally, you must demonstrate an analytical, objective and dispassionate style, so emotive comments about your own organisation (though often entertaining) will be unwelcome, especially as they suggest an immaturity of perspective and a lack of 'political' sophistication.

- Moreover, the examiners expect you to be able to make intelligent use of your own work experiences whilst simultaneously showing that you are adequately familiar with the practices of people management in economic/business sectors other than the one in which you are currently employed. This means, too, that you should be able to identify some enterprises that are 'world class' in terms of their people-management processes, the commitment that their people exhibit so far as their organisations are concerned, and the supreme quality of their people-related outputs. Such organisations (at the time of writing) will include Tesco, First Direct, the RAC, Singapore Airlines, Nokia, Microsoft, and Pret A Manger. It's worth noting that most of these organisations manage people in unconventional ways not always described in textbooks – but that is one of the characteristics that makes these organisations so special. Capturing the unconventional is as important for your learning as recording the systematic – remember the important distinction here between *infrastructure* and *differentiators*.

- Finally, please take your assignment seriously. It is an important aspect of the learning process in itself, but your assignment mark can become crucial if you obtain a marginal fail (45–49) mark in the examination and your case for moderation/ condonement is being evaluated by the examiners.

Quite commonly it is believed that the operation of 'luck' has something to do with examination success in this and other subjects. At the margin, that is probably true, particularly if you have adopted a 'satisficing' strategy as described above. However, the CIPD examinations are specifically designed to reduce and even eliminate any element of 'luck', by asking a broad range of questions and by promoting a balance between 'theory', 'practice' and 'application'. If you conscientiously pursue the preparation guidelines discussed here, then 'luck' won't come into it: you will succeed, and you will thoroughly deserve to do so.

3 EXAMINER'S INSIGHTS

First, it may be helpful to outline the descriptive commentaries that are used by the chief examiner when assessing the scripts for Managing People, because this will emphasise the elements that produce marks and the 'mistakes' made by candidates that prevent marks from being awarded (note that it is not possible to 'lose' marks: marks are either awarded or they are not, but they are never taken away because of, say, some foolish mistake).

Positive descriptive commentaries

- Demonstrates business orientation through a good understanding of people strategies, recognising that people are meant to be contributors to organisational success.

- Appears sensitive to wider 'political' and organisational issues.

- Equipped with application capability, generating proposals for action that are cogent, specific and convincing.

- Produces some recommendations that reveal evidence of original and innovative thinking.

- Confronts implementation problems, that is, indicates how 'big picture' recommendations can be translated into tangible and operational actions.

- Shows thorough knowledge of the subject matter.

- Reinforces knowledge with critical understanding and the willingness to challenge research, textbook generalisations and/or conventional wisdom.

- Includes third-party references to relevant literature, research evidence and so forth.

- Draws on appropriate organisational examples to show good practice and/or 'world-class' benchmarking possibilities.

- Makes constructive use of own work experiences in analytical, learning fashion.

- Answers are well presented and persuasive, lucid and articulate.

Negative descriptive commentaries

- Absence of business orientation, with answers that appear to put people first without any priority for organisational goals and purposes.

- No coherent application capability, but instead relies on general platitudes and undeveloped ideas.

- Knowledge of subject-matter poor, with a mixture of straightforward ignorance and significant factual mistakes.

- No evidence of critical understanding, producing answers largely confined to superficial and simplistic description.

- Few or no references to relevant third-party evidence and/or organisational examples.

- Persuasion and presentation poor: arguments difficult to follow, material hard to read, unelaborated bullet points.

- Answers typically too discursive and unfocused, betraying lack of awareness about the key issues to be addressed.

Second, scrutiny of the scripts presented for the May 2003 diet has yielded the somewhat depressing conclusion that although there appears to have been some acceptance of the 'new' performance criteria linked to the Professional Development Scheme, the causes for poor performance are no different from the causes that have been discussed in a long succession of reports by this chief examiner.

Many candidates take too long before getting to the point of the question – and therefore the central point of the answer. This can mean that some students do not have sufficient time to produce material that can qualify for marks, especially in Section B, where time is of the essence. It should be clearly understood that the chief examiner and his or her colleagues do not take account of the quantity of text produced, but look instead at its quality, relevance to the issue, business orientation and strategic comprehension.

Even now it remains true that the majority of scripts make no references whatsoever to any third-party sources of evidence, organisational benchmarking or work-related experiences. Yet it is virtually impossible to pass any of the PDS subjects without such references, given that they add authenticity and conviction to statements that are otherwise unsupported by any empirical justification. Many students do not even show that they have read any of the basic textbooks.

Within Section A, it is common for each of the alternative questions to have two sub-questions, one asking for critical evaluation and the other for application potential to be discussed in 'your own organisation' (or another organisation of your choice, as outlined in the rubric). In a small but significant number of instances, responses to the second sub-question – the 'application' part – contain no references to any real organisation at all, but discuss instead what 'an organisation' should or should not do. This is not acceptable. If anyone entering the Managing People examination is not in gainful employment, or lacks any personal work-related experiences, then strenuous efforts must be made to compensate for this deficiency, perhaps by seeking assistance from the nearest CIPD branch, by soliciting co-operation from appropriate friends (including fellow students) and relatives, or by diligently reading as much as possible about the authentic world of work from relevant periodicals like *People Management*.

At the other extreme, a few candidates addressed virtually every question in the whole paper with examples from a single enterprise, this presumably being the organisation that employed the candidate. In many cases, too, the coverage was exclusively descriptive and anecdotal, instead of being (constructively) analytical and critical; often it was glib, superficial and simplistic, so that, for instance, corporate claims about 'our people are our greatest asset' were reproduced without comment and certainly without any substantive evidence that could enable the reader to judge the truth of such assertions for him or herself. It is important to understand that the purpose of the CIPD examinations (including Managing People) is not principally to improve the performance of the candidate in whatever role they happen to occupy currently, but rather to prepare people for a professional future across a variety of organisational types and economic sectors – and so breadth of learning should be a significant part of the learning process and must equally be exhibited in examination answers.

A further general difficulty concerns the tendency to reproduce highly coloured statements and rhetoric about the importance of people, as if any commitment by candidates to the underpinning values of Managing People will automatically ensure the award of sufficient marks, without the necessity for any hard facts and evidence. Anyone holding such views, however tenuously or subconsciously, must dispose of them straight away. In the vast majority of organisations, especially those that are commercially motivated, people management is not an act of faith but a financial calculation based on cost/benefit analysis.

Finally, the chief examiner finds it regrettable that students sometimes portray attitudes characterised by political naivety. Conflicts inside organisations, and between organisational functions, are a fact of life (though not necessarily to be welcomed), and the idea that all the employees in an enterprise might be selflessly dedicated to the organisation's mission and vision is one that is seldom attained in practice. Nor is it likely that one can trace straightforward cause/effect relationships between, say, job enrichment and employee retention; and it is certainly not the case that 'world-class' levels of achievement can be achieved solely through the creation of appropriate people-management systems. Getting the best out of people is both an 'art' and a 'science': the systems are derived from the 'science', but the 'art' is what makes the real difference.

By contrast, the scripts receiving a distinction have all displayed the following features:

- Questions are answered in a very specific, very focused way, with a concentration on the essentials. Words are not wasted, digressions not introduced, and questions themselves are not repeated within the answers.

- Scripts incorporate references to third-party literature, research, CIPD materials and reports, *People Management* articles, and other relevant, authoritative sources of facts, ideas and thinking.

- Distinction students write analytically but constructively about their own organisations. If they reproduce any corporate rhetoric, they are sufficiently detached about it to mention some of its limitations and the fact that it is not always translated into reality through everyday organisational experience. They acknowledge that leaders, managers and people have flaws – sometimes, indeed, they are manipulative, deceitful and exploitative.

- Answers actively demonstrate that their authors have knowledge about sectors other than their own, so the people concerned have read widely and taken the trouble to open their intellects to the possibility that things may be done in new and original ways.

- Answers are cogently structured, reader-friendly, professional, well presented and organised. Above all, they are easily legible.

- Time is allocated efficiently so that marks are spread throughout Section A and across all seven answers for Section B.

The above recipe is not utopian and unattainable – the fact that some candidates can attain it merely suggests to the chief examiner that others could as well. I hope that this belief is vindicated by the results to be achieved in the future, when you take the examination for Managing People.

SECTION 3

EXAMINATION PRACTICE AND FEEDBACK

4 MANAGING PEOPLE FEEDBACK ON EXAMINATION QUESTIONS

Introduction

The purpose of this chapter is to provide some advice and guidance on tackling Section A and Section B questions. It should be noted, however, that this feedback does not constitute model answers. The reality of organisational life, especially when dealing with people, means that there can be no ready-made, prescriptive, one-size-fits-all solutions to dealing with organisational problems and managing people. The HR professional needs to be able to respond to organisational issues in a way that reflects the CIPD vision of 'business partner' and 'thinking performer'. This means displaying in examination answers judgements and solutions that reflect a business orientation; knowledge of wider organisational practice; recent research findings; knowledge of the subject matter of managing people and the ability to apply this within specific organisational contexts; and the ability to present arguments in a coherent and convincing manner. For these reasons there can be no prescriptive, standardised or 'right' responses.

Guidance is provided on three past papers and the approach adopted is slightly different for each paper. For the May 2003 paper a full and detailed response is provided to both Section A and Section B questions. It is appreciated that within the time constraints of the examination candidates would not necessarily be able to go into this amount of detail or produce answers of this length. The aim here, however, is to provide an indication of the nature and scope of research and third party citations that might be used to support answers. As the chief examiner has made clear in feedback reports, it is expected that students will be familiar with the majority of significant CIPD research and will be required to include a convincing number of references to research to justify the high profile given to evidence-based argument. Candidates should, for example, be familiar with studies such as that of John Purcell (Purcell *et al* 2003b), which explores the link between HR practices and organisational performance that is central to Managing People.

Coverage of the November 2003 paper is shorter and focused on guidelines for interpreting the question and structuring answers. The aim here is to highlight the vital importance of focusing on the question and not answering a question the candidate might like to have been set or padding out answers with irrelevant material. Coverage of the May 2004 paper comprises examples of actual answers from candidates' scripts.

Throughout the feedback, reference is made to examples of world-class organisations that are known for the quality of their HRM and that seek to optimise the contribution that managing people can make to organisational performance. Increasingly, questions in the Managing People exam will concentrate on the mechanisms that enable organisations to deliver high performance and commitment from the people they employ. These mechanisms go well beyond the establishment of infrastructure systems, processes, procedures and ethical/legal compliance. What differentiates organisations like Tesco, Nationwide, BMW and First Direct is the way in which people managers adopt and embed an aspirational vision.

May 2003 Section A

Question I

Read the following material, taken from Stephen Taylor, *People resourcing* (London: CIPD, 2002, 2nd edition, p. 398), and answer the questions beneath.

At the Sears Group in the USA, over a period of some years, a great deal of data was collected by task forces concerning employee development and team working, customer needs and satisfaction, and revenue growth, sales per square foot and other financial measures. Central was the way that the company sought to capture 'soft issues' such as staff satisfaction using hard measurements. This was done through the use of questionnaire surveys. Correlations were then made between changes in the P&D [personnel and development] indicators and improvements in the financial performance of different business units (i.e., benchmarking). The analysis allowed the company to make the following statement: 'a five point improvement in employee attitudes will drive a 1.3 point improvement in customer satisfaction which in turn will lead to a 0.5 per cent improvement in revenue growth.'

(a) *Comment on this research, including the conclusions and the methodologies employed. How can such studies be made totally credible and robust?*
(b) *How do the findings at the Sears Group compare with other studies that have sought to demonstrate a link between people management and organisational outcomes?*

This question addresses a topical and ongoing issue – that of the relationship between employee performance and corporate profitability.

As the passage from Taylor's book makes clear, the Sears Group adopted a hard, quantitative approach to measuring the people and development contribution to organisational effectiveness and performance. This approach reflects the concept of human capital, a term originally developed by economists to describe the value created by people and other intangible assets within an organisation. The concept of human capital sees people as a vital corporate investment and source of corporate profits.

Establishing a methodology for the value that people management practices create for the organisation poses an opportunity for demonstrating the strategic credentials of HR. Hard measures, such as statistical correlations between aspects of people management practice and profit, shareholder value and revenue growth have the advantage that they appear objective and can often be expressed simply, as in the extract, where a direct and causal relationship is suggested between employee satisfaction and revenue growth. However, there are conceptual and methodological problems with adopting a hard, quantitative approach. These include:

1. The underlying assumption behind such approaches is that value can only be added in financial terms. Adopting an accounting

terminology and attempting to quantify the people management contribution conforms to a prevailing accountancy view of how organisations and organisational processes should be managed. It leaves the HR function vulnerable to outsourcing based solely on an evaluation of what people management practices exist and how much these cost.

2.   The effectiveness of people management practices on organisational performance is difficult to measure. People are not passive, compliant assets and human behaviour cannot be readily predicted. Feelings, attitudes, opinions, emotions and behaviours cannot be easily quantified, reliably counted and uniformly measured. Adopting a hard, quantitative approach is too simplistic and can undermine the people contribution.

3.   The methodology for putting numbers behind people assets is questionable and incompletely developed. No standard measures exist. As the extract shows, the Sears Group used hard measures to measure soft issues such as employee development, team working and employee satisfaction. Other studies attempt to measure flexibility and job security or the use of incentives and to link these to organisational performance. The measures used are variable and, as a result, it is difficult to draw general conclusions. The selection of the measures used is also subject to qualitative interpretation as judgement may be required as to which criteria are relevant. Moreover, despite the increasing sophistication of research and statistical analysis suggesting causality between people management and organisational performance, there is no established link. Statistical correlations do not prove causality and other variables may impact on organisational performance. It is both simplistic and questionable to suggest, for example, that flexible working increases profits.

4.   There are also practical problems in collecting reliable and meaningful information. As the extract shows, the Sears Group relied on gathering information through questionnaires but the validity and reliability of information gathered through questionnaires can be affected by the self-awareness and honesty of respondents. Attitude surveys can be misleading if poorly

designed. It may also be possible that the costs of collecting and analysing certain sets of information may not be justified by the benefits in the shape of improved performance. A further problem may be that the methodology for working out how different people management practices impact on organisational performance is only possible within large organisations, such as the Sears Group, with a wealth of different practices to analyse and measure.

In recent years there has been considerable research focused on attempting to demonstrate a link between people management practices and improved organisational outcomes. The US academic Mark Huselid (1995) has undertaken research based on large-scale surveys of HR practice in top American companies and compared this with data on their economic and market performance. His findings have suggested a link between what he termed 'high performance work practices' (such as sophisticated recruitment and selection, formal information sharing, job design, performance appraisal) and business performance. Huselid used company market value as the key indicator of business performance, and found that firms with significantly above average scores on an index of high work practices provided an extra market value of between £10,000 and £40,000. The key to achieving such benefits, he argued, was not in the adoption of specific people management practices but in developing the right combination or 'bundle' of practices. The integration of people management practice with other business strategies was thus an important feature of organisational performance. A study by Pfeffer (1998) identified seven HR techniques and linked these to shareholder value. According to Pfeffer, companies that emphasised employment security, put maximum resources into recruiting the right people, used self-managed teams and decentralised management, linked high wages to organisational performance, invested in training, reduced status differentials and were willing to share information stood to increase shareholder value by between $20,000 and $40,000 per employee.

The work of US academics has been supplemented by British studies. Most recently the study by Purcell *et al* (2003b) examined the impact of people management on organisational performance, commonly referred to as the 'black box' problem. The study was undertaken over 30 months in 12 organisations from a wide range of sectors, and produced a model linking people and performance. In essence, the model suggests that people perform well when they possess the necessary skills and knowledge; when they have the motivation to perform; and when they are given the opportunity. The study identified a range of HR policies and practices necessary to support the ability + motivation + opportunity (AMO) framework. However, the findings from the study demonstrated that two additional elements were necessary in the people performance link. The first is the existence of a 'big idea' or a clear mission underpinned by values and a culture expressing what the organisation stands for and is trying to achieve (for example, mutuality at Nationwide, quality at Jaguar); the second is the crucial role of line management in implementing and enacting HR policies.

Academic studies that have established a link between the management of people and organisational performance have been supplemented by the work of consultants attempting to produce a model incorporating concrete measures quantifying the value of people management practices. Arthur Andersen have adopted the balanced scorecard approach first developed by Kaplan and Norton (1996). The scorecard comprises a set of performance measures in four areas – customer (for example, customer satisfaction and retention, new customers, market share), financial (for example, profitability, cash flow, sales growth), internal business process (for example, innovation, existing and new processes to be mastered to meet financial and customer objectives) and learning and growth (for example, organisational structure, employee satisfaction, skills and retention). Consultants Watson Wyatt have produced a Human Capital Index whereby firms are given a score depending on their total return to shareholders and ability to create value beyond their physical assets (www.watsonwyatt.com). The index highlights key HR practices that correspond to shareholder gains – excellence in recruiting, clear rewards and accountability, flexible workplace, communications integrity. The Business Excellence model also provides a template for linking business outputs (results) and organisational inputs (for example, leadership and people management practices).

Question 2

Read the following material, extracted from an article ('Wakey wakey') by Gerwyn Davies in *Financial World* (December 2002), and answer the questions beneath.

In *The motivation handbook* (published by the CIPD), authors Sally Hollyforde and Steve Whiddett say that because motivation is personal, organisations cannot impose it. A manager's job, they say, is to understand each person's expectations of, and contribution to, the company, regardless of where they are in the workplace hierarchy. A good manager will be able to use that understanding in order to motivate.

The article concludes with a list of nine 'Motivational Practices':

1. Give people responsibility for the outcomes of their work
2. Set clear and realistic goals
3. Ensure that people have the resources to do their job
4. Provide unambiguous and honest feedback
5. Give credit where credit is due and make sure it is known within the team
6. Provide learning and development opportunities
7. Implement reward packages that reflect the job and the external market rate
8. Create an environment governed by fairness and respect
9. Create a happy workplace

(a) To what extent are the views about motivation at work expressed here consistent with research findings on the subject?

(b) Evaluate your own work environment and organisation against the nine 'Motivational Practices' outlined in the article. What changes would be desirable?

This question reflects the fact that work and attitudes to work have changed considerably. Work remains a fundamental aspect of people's lives but whilst many are satisfied with the work they do, many are not. Evidence as to the quality of working life is mixed and generalisations are difficult. For example, research by the Policy Studies Institute (see White 2000) found that the proportion of people who felt completely satisfied with their work fell from 52 to 45 per cent between 1992 and 2000. The ESRC 2000 Employment Survey found that work intensification, greater control and surveillance and long hours were key factors contributing to lower levels of job satisfaction and personal commitment to the organisation, especially among those with higher levels of education. However, by contrast, research by Guest (2001) reported that job satisfaction within the private sector rose between 1998 and 2001. The question thus calls for an awareness of the impact of organisational change on the employment relationship and recognition that patterns of workplace change affect different people in different ways. It requires an informed awareness of research into motivation at work that goes beyond that of the content theories of Maslow, Herzberg and McGregor. Consideration of studies of the practice and effectiveness of empowerment would be particularly relevant.

The concept of empowerment suggests that employees at all levels in the organisation are responsible and accountable for their actions and should be given the responsibility and authority to make decisions about their work. Empowerment implies the ability to communicate, to learn, to exercise initiative, to solve problems, to work independently or in teams. However, empowerment needs to be analysed within a broader context of organisational practice. The reality for many employees has been a widening gap between the rhetoric of empowerment and the reality of work intensification, increased organisational stress and insecurity at work. The effects of change, organisational restructuring and increased insecurity invariably generate a tendency to 'play it safe', to 'keep your head down' – hardly empowered behaviours. Moreover, as Wilkinson (2001) suggests, employees empowered to take decisions are sceptical and unwilling to use their discretion if they feel constantly under the scrutiny of managers. Few organisations have created conditions that are conducive to empowerment and much of the evidence suggests that organisations have adopted a piecemeal, ad hoc approach to empowerment rather than taking an integrated and holistic approach.

Another relevant concept in discussing motivation at work is that of the psychological contract, or the expectations that employees have of the organisation in terms of their contribution and what they can expect in return. In the context of large-scale change the critical issue becomes how change affects discretionary behaviour and the choices individuals make about how they work. Herriot and Pemberton (1995) have argued that the psychological contract for many employees has changed fundamentally. Whereas the traditional psychological contract was based on long-term commitment, security and steady progression through the organisational hierarchy, the 'new' psychological contract is more transactional and based on short-term, flexible arrangements and the offer of employability. Research (for example, Coyle-Shapiro and Kessler 2000) has shown that when employees perceive that the organisation has breached their psychological contract, or their expectations about work and progression, they feel less committed to the organisation. In such circumstances job satisfaction also dips.

The second part of the question calls for a critical evaluation of the motivational practices used within the candidate's organisation. Many organisations are likely to be deficient against at least some of the motivational practices listed and a balanced, informed and constructive analysis is called for. Answers should avoid being negatively destructive but should equally avoid merely repeating corporate rhetoric about people as an organisational asset. In addition to analysing organisational practice against the areas identified, answers should provide positive, constructive and cost-effective proposals for improvement. Many remedies such as management recognition and appreciation for effective performance cost nothing but can be powerful motivators.

Question 3

Read the following material, taken from *The elephant and the flea: looking backwards to the future* by Charles Handy (Hutchinson, 2001) and answer the questions beneath.

In this extract, Handy is congratulating himself on the foresight displayed in his 1981 predictions about the future nature of the UK workforce and the nature of work itself.

It had been foolhardy then to prophesy that by the year 2000 less than half the working population would be in conventional full-time jobs on what are called 'indefinite period contracts'. The rest of us would either be self-employed, or part-timers, perhaps temps of one sort or another, or out of paid work altogether. We would need, I said, a portfolio of different bits and pieces of paid work, or a collection of clients and customers, if we wanted to earn a living. As it turned out, by the year 2000 the British labour force on those indefinite period contracts in full-time employment had fallen to 40 per cent, and the BBC World Service was running programmes on the theme 'What Future for Men?'

(a)   *To what extent does the evidence support Handy's claims, with particular reference to the emergence of flexible working, the spread of portfolio working, and the continued existence of conventional full-time employment?*

(b)   *Outline and justify your own predictions about the nature of the UK workforce 20 years from now.*

The labour market has changed significantly in the time since Handy made his predictions but not in the ways he suggests. The latest research evidence does not support Handy's view that the number of people in employment with 'indefinite period contracts' is increasing. Neither is there evidence that the types of jobs being created are predominantly part-time and temporary.

The ESRC 2000 Employment Survey (part of a wider research programme entitled Future of Work), points to relative stability in the workplace and challenges commonly held views of widespread flexibility and radical developments in non-standard forms of working. Full-time working is still the norm and there has been a growth in permanent employment, rather than a contraction. The level of self-employment grew throughout the 1980s but has barely changed over the last decade. There is no evidence of an increase in the number of people working for shorter periods with a wider number of employers and many people still regard their job as part of a career with distinct promotion prospects. The concept of the 'portfolio' worker remains the exception and portfolio workers are more likely to be the casualties of corporate restructuring than a new breed of entrepreneur although there has been significant growth in the use of interim managers in employment, within both private and public sectors, a category not anticipated by Handy in 1981. Female activity rates have increased and the proportion of women in the labour force accounts for 46 per cent of total employment. However, labour markets remain heavily segmented with women concentrated in the service sector and in lower level jobs. The proportion of women in managerial, executive and board level roles has increased only marginally. There is certainly no evidence to suggest, as Handy does, a gender balance revolution in job creation.

Relevant sources of information in relation to labour market trends include the Office for National Statistics (www.statistics.gov.uk) and Taylor (2000).

Making predictions about future labour market characteristics and trends provided candidates with considerable scope. However, predictions should be realistic, justified and defensible. Continuity is as relevant as change and given the gradual and incremental change in labour markets over the last 20 years, it would be reasonable to expect such changes to continue. As a result we might expect to see a steady increase in the growth of non-standard employment, a continuing de-industrialisation of the UK economy and shift from manufacturing to service sector employment, and changes in the demographic composition of the labour force. Public sector employment has also declined significantly in recent years. Structural changes in employment are likely to become embedded as the United Kingdom becomes a predominantly service and information based economy.

Self-employment, flexible and part-time working offer personal freedom to combine work with other commitments but the downside is that a greater proportion of low paid, low skilled jobs are undertaken by women, school leavers, students and older workers. Future change in this scenario might mean that some types of work (for example low-level, customer-facing jobs such as supermarket checkout operators and some call centre functions) disappear and are replaced by automated systems. More conspicuous change might relate to the nature of work itself as a result of technological change and the development of Internet technologies.

The casualisation of jobs in sectors such as retail and hotel and catering is likely to result in strengthened political pressures for a higher national minimum wage. Long-term careers in large organisations are likely to decline as employees are forced to move between companies. Forthcoming decades are also likely to see pressures on the labour market because of an ageing population with consequent demands to lift the retirement age. The past decade has also seen the UK labour market move from labour surplus to labour

shortage and a reduction in structural unemployment. Future
increases in the employment rate will depend on organisations
making better use of this potential reserve of labour supply.

May 2003 Section B

> You should assume that you have just arrived at your work-
> station and switched on your PC. The following 10 e-mail
> messages appear. You are required to indicate the *content* of your
> responses to any SEVEN of them; the *manner* of your response
> (whether by an e-mail reply, or a face-to-face conversation, a
> phone call, etc) is not relevant.

Question I

> *From the IT Manager*: We employ a large proportion of temps in
> our department. Their attitudes are too instrumental – what
> could we learn from other organisations about ways to increase
> their commitment to our organisation and its goals?

In answering this question candidates should demonstrate that they
understand the term 'instrumental' and how this is reflected in
employee behaviour. Employees with an instrumental orientation to
work see work not as a central issue but rather as a means to an end.
The basis of temporary work contributes to an instrumental orientation in that, until recently, many temporary staff received less
favourable treatment and had no rights to join occupational pension
schemes or access to benefits available to permanent staff. The very
nature of their employment status makes their employment insecure. Such factors impact the levels of trust, loyalty and commitment
of temporary staff to the organisation. Temporary workers may be
less reliable, have higher levels of turnover, unwilling to work
beyond contract or the specific requirements of their job role and
motivated solely by financial concerns. Such aspects of behaviour
are not surprising given that reliability, stability and discretionary
behaviour are linked to employee commitment and with temporary
staff the nature of that commitment is transient.

The challenge for the organisation is therefore to encourage discretionary behaviour whilst retaining the flexibility that temporary workers allow. One way of achieving this is to attempt to integrate temporary staff into the organisation as far as possible and to remove obvious distinctions between temporary and permanent staff. Temporary employees should be involved in any team building activities and recognised and rewarded in the same way as permanent staff. They should be involved in team briefing activities and other communication exercises that seek to increase employee loyalty and commitment. If uniforms are worn, these should also be provided for temporary workers. Making the organisation a great place to work with supportive and effective managers will increase the commitment of all employees including temporary staff. Recent legislation designed to improve the status of temporary staff will help although it may also serve to deter some organisations from using temporary staff to the same degree.

Question 2

> *From the Research Manager*: Forgive my cynicism, but I am sceptical of presentations made at conferences by individuals who tell us about the success of some radically different people management approaches developed in a single organisation. What is the evidence to show that such approaches (even if as successful as the speakers claim) could be easily adopted by other organisations?

This question required candidates to discuss the work of a range of authors who argue that there are a number of basic underlying philosophies which result in the successful management of people, lead to improved work performance and to organisational success. It also calls for a critical appraisal of the transferability of such approaches. Different approaches were possible.

Answers might have drawn on specific cases of remarkable management practices in a single enterprise. Here a leading example has been Semco (Semler 1993), a flourishing Brazilian manufacturing company. Semco is a single-status, democratic workplace with only four grades of staff, no dress code, no segregated parking or dining, no job titles, no job specifications or other formalities common to large organisations. Managers and employees are empowered to work in their own way and to take decisions. Workers set their own working hours, schedules and production targets. They are responsible for product quality, for implementing improvements and appraising the performance of managers. Another example is Capital One, a highly successful US financial services company, where the focus is on constant experimentation and review. Employees are encouraged to compete for resources, to select the project teams they join, lobby senior managers with ideas and generally to organise themselves in whatever way is most appropriate for them.

An alternative approach might have been to critically evaluate the so-called 'excellence' movement that associated the success of leading edge, 'excellent' companies with the improved motivation of people through involved management styles. The 'excellence' authors (for example, Peters and Waterman 1982) argued that people were the most valuable resource of any organisation and that training and developing them, adequately rewarding them, involving them in organisational policy making, especially at the customer interface level, resulted in enhanced motivation and organisational performance. More recently, Pfeffer (1998) has argued that people are at the heart of business success and that seven HR policies (employment security; careful recruitment; team work and decentralised management; high pay with an incentive element; extensive training; narrow status differentials; developed communications mechanisms) are common to high performing organisations, almost irrespective of culture.

Pfeffer's approach and that of the 'excellence' writers generally has been criticised on the grounds of advocating a 'best practice' approach to the management of people rather than tailoring HR practice to the organisation's specific situation and environment. In discussing the transferability of people management practice, relevant concepts to draw on would be those of cultural difference and contingency.

Answers should therefore acknowledge the methodological and conceptual limitations of the 'excellence' literature but nevertheless recognise the contribution it has made to highlighting a compelling case for the human aspects of the enterprise. As Pfeffer (1998) suggests, so few organisations apply the complete set of HR practices that there remains considerable room for improvement and management scepticism of so-called 'radically' different people management practices may conceal a resistance to change.

Question 3

From the Learning and Development Manager: What does research tell us about the behavioural reasons why performance appraisal is so problematic? After all, the idea of appraisal sounds so attractive, in theory.

This question is focused on the behavioural reasons whereby the effectiveness of performance appraisal can be undermined. Answers that focused on design, structural or procedural aspects would therefore have missed the point of the question. There are a wide variety of behavioural reasons why performance appraisal is problematic.

Subjectivity and bias are inherent problems in performance appraisal because prejudice and stereotyping can cloud objectivity of assessment, prevent an analytical evaluation of performance and distort the overall assessment. Redman (2001) summarises the distorting effects of performance appraisal as:

- halo and horns effect where positive or negative aspects dominate the appraisal rating

- doppelganger effect where the appraisal rating reflects the similarity between appraisers and appraised

- crony effect where the overall assessment is distorted by the closeness of the relationship between appraisers and appraised

- Veblen effect where all those appraised receive middle-order ratings irrespective of their performance

- impression effect where assessments may be distorted by the effectiveness of employees in managing their reputations and creating a favourable impression of their performance although their actual performance outcomes may be less impressive.

Rowe (1986) highlighted problems arising from the application of perceptual processes in rating performance, and identified a number of problems arising from unfair bias in managerial assessment of performance. These included tendencies to give undue weight to recent events which impacted on performance (both positive and negative); to avoid giving low ratings, even when appropriate, for fear of upsetting the employee; not giving high ratings on principle; giving a poor overall rating on the basis of poor performance in a particular area; rating performance as good or satisfactory rather than using the end points of rating scales.

Managers may also manipulate performance ratings for a variety of reasons. Longenecker (1989) found that managers would reduce ratings to 'punish' a difficult employee, to 'scare' an employee into better performance or to reinforce their own authority.

Question 4

> *From the Accounts Manager*: Reading my *Financial Times* the other day, I saw an article in which it was argued that it is important 'to understand our employees as whole individuals and engage effectively with them on that basis'. Why should we? I always tell my people to leave their personal problems at home, and thus far it seems to have worked.

Responses to the question of treating employees as 'whole individuals' should recognise that asking people to separate out their work and home lives is neither helpful nor realistic. At a general level, it can be argued that employers who allow staff to dovetail work with family and personal commitments stand to gain a more motivated, committed, efficient and productive workforce. Such approaches are compatible with treating employees as assets to be nurtured and invested in. More specifically, poor performance at work can have a variety of causes. As Weightman (2004, p187) suggests, performance problems can stem from a variety of personal, organisational and individual characteristics and diagnosing the reasons behind a performance gap is necessary in identifying appropriate strategies and remedies for rectifying performance problems.

Answers to this question might also consider the business case for family friendly policies and recognise that a key feature of high performing organisations is that they take account of their employees as people. Answers should, ideally, be illustrated by references to case studies of organisations who have addressed the issue of work/life balance in relation to their business needs. IDS Study 698 (2000) presents case studies of six organisations that have addressed issues around the work/life balance of employees in relation to business needs. Fox's Biscuits has sought to apply flexibility to shift working to enable employees to meet their personal responsibilities and commitments whilst meeting production targets and schedules. Arthur Andersen, as providers of professional services, can offer considerable flexibility to accountants and consultants provided their overall output is unaffected. The trade-off here involves the creation of a work/life balance framework that incorporates the need to work long hours on occasions to meet client needs. Lloyds TSB conducted feasibility studies in treating employees as assets and becoming an employer of choice which found that for men and women, finding the right balance between work and home could be the most critical factor in deciding whether or not to move to a different organisation. As a result, Lloyds TSB launched Work Options, a formal flexible working scheme in 1999. The scheme is open to all staff and places no restriction on patterns of work employees may choose, they have only to show that these will not be detrimental to the business.

Question 5

From the Customer Services Manager: A management writer once said, 'Listen to your employees. Do what they tell you.' Is this good advice? Why don't we do it more in our organisation?

From a managerial perspective, doing 'what employees tell you' suggests an abdication of managerial prerogative and acquiescence to employee pressure that may be unwise and inappropriate. Those organisations that have established reputations for sustained and superior performance, for example, First Direct, Tesco, Richer Sounds, Pret A Manger, have done so principally because of their visionary, top-down leadership. Leadership within such organisations has assessed the needs of the organisation and translated this into plans of action to build sustainable success through integrated and appropriately applied people management strategies and practices which have been customised to organisational circumstances.

Such organisations have managed to successfully and productively integrate employee involvement and participation but organisational success has been built upon the articulation of a clear, ambitious and aspirational vision from the leadership rather than from bottom-up employee involvement.

Responses to this question should therefore demonstrate awareness and appreciation of the characteristics and attributes of aspirational leadership. As Purcell's (Purcell *et al* 2003a, 2003b) work has shown creating an effective vision and direction for the organisation is a key critical element of leadership because it energises commitment by providing a compelling rationale to direct effort. In addition to providing a strategic direction, the articulation of organisational vision also represents organisational values and ideals.

Responses should be illustrated by reference to case studies where the clear articulation of organisational vision and aspirational leadership has resulted in superior organisational performance. For example, Richer Sounds is the biggest and most profitable hi-fi retailer in the country with the highest sales per square foot of any retailer in the world. Julian Richer argues that it is possible to achieve strong central control and empowerment and that effective leadership is about achieving the right balance between control and motivation. Staff are set clear standards and robust procedures. All employees are engaged in continuous improvement through learning. Reward systems are aligned to behaviours that the organisation values and wishes to encourage, such as innovation and outstanding customer service. To emphasise the importance of customer satisfaction to business success, staff are given a degree of freedom in using their initiative to ensure customer needs are met. Bureaucracy is kept to a minimum so that prompt action 'delights' the customer.

Question 6

From an independent research organisation: We are undertaking a study into the causes of the lower levels of job satisfaction frequently experienced by people working in the public sector. What do you think are the causes of this? What is the solution?

A number of indicators point to lower levels of job satisfaction by public sector employees. For example, despite the existence of strong absence management policies, absence levels are rising and are considerably higher than in the private sector (CIPD 2002). Stress levels in the public sector are also higher with the highest levels reported in the NHS and local government (CIPD 2003).

Lower levels of job satisfaction by public sector employees can be attributed to a variety of causes. Public sector organisations have experienced considerable change. Most state run corporations have been privatised (telecommunications, utilities) and state-run services (for instance, NHS, the educational system) have been required to operate along more commercial lines. Restructuring and the introduction of market-driven reforms has prompted far-reaching reforms of employment and management practice and public sector work is increasingly carried out under some form of sub-contracting or franchising arrangement.

Despite market driven reforms, however, public sector decision-making remains inherently political. Government influence, the legal framework of public policy and public scrutiny of the quality of public sector service delivery has increased in intensity as a result of the introduction of league tables publicising poorly performing schools, hospitals and local authorities. Managerial decision-making and employment practice is thus subject to a wide variety of legal, political and economic constraints and influenced by a multiplicity of stakeholders. Customer expectations of public sector services have also been transformed with customers expecting high quality services and standards that are 'joined up' across different agencies and public bodies. There are additional expectations that public sector services should be responsive and utilise appropriate forms of electronic delivery. Contextual and structural change has contributed to initiative overload and 'change fatigue'.

In addition to the nature, scope and extent of public sector transformation other relevant factors impacting on levels of job satisfaction could include: the public sector's characteristic pattern of organisation into functional hierarchies which creates systemic and cultural blockages to change; the absence of a clear aspirational vision of the future; media scrutiny and criticism for misuse of funds; lack of coherence in different initiatives intended to improve service delivery; low pay; a greater presence of marginal employees with lower levels of organisational commitment.

Whilst the problems of the public sector may be readily identified, the solutions are perhaps less obvious, particularly given the scale of the modernisation agenda (the NHS employs 1 million people, the Civil Service employs 500,000. Similar numbers are employed within local government, education, the police and criminal justice systems). Moreover, there is considerable variety within public sector organisations. Some are highly centralised, others have a large degree of autonomy. In some cases services are provided through third parties or voluntary agencies. As a result there can be no 'one size fits all' solution.

The government's strategy for public sector improvement has been set out in the Office of Public Sector Reform document *Reforming our public services: principles into practice*, which emphasises four key aspects of reform – setting national standards within a framework of accountability; devolving responsibility for delivery to local levels; introducing greater flexibility in meeting customer needs; and expanding public services to provide greater customer choice.

Implicit within such proposals are a greater awareness of 'customers' and the deliberate application of management practices from competitive industry; increased reliance on outsourcing; the widespread application of performance management systems; fostering a positive and receptive climate of change; breaking down barriers between public sector organisations to provide a seamless service from a variety of agencies; new styles of leadership in managing complex partnership and stakeholder groups; the development of greater levels of employee empowerment; reform of pay systems and terms and conditions of employment to allow greater flexibility to reflect local needs and priorities. Many of these proposals and initiatives are controversial and suspect in their application and answers should reflect a critical dimension.

Question 7

> *From a team leader in the Call Centre*: For my management diploma I have to do a survey and I'd appreciate it if I could include your responses in my report. Drawing on your knowledge of relevant research and of benchmark call centres, what do you think should be the key features of effective people management in such environments?

Telephone call centres have grown dramatically over the last decade and represent substantial cost savings to organisations through a rationalisation of work processes and the use of information technology. However, the design of jobs in call centres owes a great deal to scientific management. Call centre work is fragmented, closely monitored, tightly controlled, highly routinised, low skilled, stressful, poorly paid and characterised by anti-social shift patterns. Low levels of job satisfaction in call centres reflect low levels of job control, inadequate training and high levels of monitoring.

A recent IDS report (2002) of 133 call centres employing 106,000 staff found average turnover rates of 24.5 per cent (an increase of 22 per cent over 2001). The same report found average pay rates to be £12,400. Other studies have identified high levels of turnover and absence as a form of exit from working conditions viewed as unpleasant and stressful. Moreover, call centre work cannot be disembodied from the provider of such services and the way in which call centre employees express their feelings towards customers' impacts of the perceived quality of the service provided.

Key features of effective people management in call centre environments should include:

- The recruitment of people with positive, customer-oriented attitudes, personality characteristics of resilience, self-motivation, patience, persistence, problem-solving mentality. Research by Higgs and Allen (2003) with 286 call centre employees identified conscientiousness, resilience, self-motivation and sensitivity as key characteristics.

- Rigorous selection based on behavioural interviewing techniques and work-based ability tests.

- Systematic socialisation and training.

- Job design techniques that reduce monotony, increase variety and enable staff to develop customer relationships by focusing on outputs rather than process measures such as call duration. Holman's (2002) study of 500 call centre agents in three call centres in the financial services sector found that staff well-being and satisfaction was associated with high employee control over working methods, low levels of monitoring and supportive team leaders. The implication here is that managers should provide a challenging work environment with scope for task variety and use monitoring as a development tool rather than as a form of control.

- The development of supportive, people-oriented team leaders and managers. Studies have highlighted the pivotal role of team leaders in improving employee well-being and maintaining motivation and morale of call centre staff (Armistead *et al* 2002).

- Team building activities and the encouragement of constructive inter-team competition.

- Attention to working conditions and 'hygiene' factors to reduce job dissatisfaction

- Reward and recognition schemes that impartially recognise achievement and progress.

Batt and Moynihan's (2002) study linked a high involvement HR strategy (high skill levels, team working, investment in training, job security) with low turnover, faster sales growth and increased knowledge sharing in call centres. An IDS report (2002) based on an examination of 133 call centres found that a significant number of organisations had introduced a number of initiatives aimed at improving staff retention. These included improved recruitment and selection techniques; the introduction of incentive schemes, flexibility of working and career progression programmes; increased training and development activities and improved communications mechanisms; improvements to the work environment. However, few mentioned job design initiatives or any significant changes to the work itself.

Question 8

From the Production Manager: Something I read the other day made me think. Apparently 'job avoidance' (increased absence, lateness, reduced effort or quality of work) is being used by dissatisfied employees as a substitute for leaving the organisation. What I want to know is: does research support this idea? Where 'job avoidance' behaviour occurs, as I think it does in my department, what could I do about it?

Job avoidance behaviour can be viewed within a wider context of employee commitment. People who are more committed to the organisation are less likely to leave. In the case of affective commitment and to a lesser degree, normative commitment, their continued presence is enthusiastic and engaged. However, continuance commitment can reflect the fact that employees remain with an organisation because they have no alternative. In such circumstances their degree of engagement may be reduced and the potential for the development of job avoidance behaviours increased.

'Job avoidance' behaviour may represent a prelude to resignation. Studies of labour turnover (for instance, Mobley 1997) have identified the psychological reasoning behind resignation and have suggested a number of distinct stages whereby job dissatisfaction can progress into resignation. At any stage in the process, the employee may re-evaluate his or her present position and decide to remain if, for example, labour market conditions are unfavourable or as a result of the perceived ease of movement. However, the employee may engage in other forms of 'withdrawal' such as absence, low productivity, lateness, poor customer service and such 'job avoidance' behaviours thus represent an indirect symptom of the employee's desire to leave.

So what can be done to eliminate 'job avoidance' behaviour and increase job satisfaction? The following courses of action might be considered:

- Investigating the factors contributing to job dissatisfaction and employee disengagement through attitude surveys, investigations into supervisor/management styles and working conditions, assessments of job design, reward and recognition schemes, absence control mechanisms and so on, and instigating improvements.

- Careful, systematic recruitment and selection practice that matches employees to tasks and responsibilities. Pret A Manger reduced turnover by 30 per cent by sharpening their recruitment and selection process and linking it to competences, and training managers to ensure that *all candidates were dealt with fairly and consistently* (Carrington 2002).

- Setting appropriate objectives, that is, targets which challenge but do not overstretch or stress and which are appropriate to the organisation and match the needs of employees. At Sun Microsystems UK, employee turnover was reduced to 4 per cent in a very competitive labour market as a result of imaginative career and development opportunities. In addition employees are provided with the systems and resources to do their jobs and identify how to provide the most professional level of service (Holbeche 1999).

- Planning development through careful design of jobs to include elements of development, delegation and empowerment where possible and appropriate.

- Keeping employees informed of departmental and organisational changes, performance standards and expectations.

- Recognising achievements and performance through appropriate financial and non-financial rewards.

Question 9

From a friend studying for the CIPD qualification: Daniel Goleman claims that EI (emotional intelligence) accounts for 85 per cent of outstanding performance in the best leaders. How does this stand up against other evidence about the components of successful leadership?

In his research of effective leaders, Goleman argues that 85 per cent of business success is due to EI and 15 per cent to cognitive ability. However, other commentators have challenged Goleman's claims and suggested that he has exaggerated the importance of EI. An effective answer to the question thus calls for reference to specific studies of leadership rather than a generalised treatment. In particular, studies that highlight the limitations of a traits/qualities approach to leadership and emphasise collaborative approaches would be relevant to the analysis.

An early but influential model of leadership was John Adair's (1982) action-centred model of leadership. Adair argued that to be effective, a leader must ensure the integration of these interrelated areas:

- achieve the task (outline objectives of the team, allocate resources, organise responsibilities)

- maintain the team (maintain morale, build team spirit, maintain cohesiveness, ensure effective communications)

- develop individuals (deal with personal problems, develop individual potential, give responsibility).

More recent studies have focused on the relationship between leaders and their teams and have highlighted more collaborative approaches to leadership as significant in ensuring organisational effectiveness. Warren Bennis (1997, 2000) in his recent books has highlighted a shift away from charismatic, individual leaders towards 'great groups', with the emphasis on creative collaboration, co-leadership and relationships. In terms of leadership, he argues, there are four major things that leaders do. One is to provide direction and meaning, the second is to generate trust, the third is to create a general sense of hope and optimism, the fourth is to act and to get results, to execute decisions as well as making them. The trust factor at work, suggests Bennis, is the social glue that keeps an organisation effective.

Alimo-Metcalfe and Alban-Metcalfe's (2003) study of leadership in public and private sector organisations has also highlighted the link between leadership behaviour and individual, team and organisational performance. Key leadership dimensions were found to be an enabling style, being accessible, being decisive and resolving complex problems.

Such studies emphasise that to be effective, leaders need to demonstrate practical competences that they can implement and that their teams will respond to.

Question 10

From the HR Director: I have to speak at a conference next month about 'Changing Attitudes to Work and what they mean for People Management'. Please let me have a few bullet points and some supporting comments for each.

Evidence of the quality of working life and attitudes to work is mixed. Some studies point to highly motivated, committed and co-operative employees whilst others suggest that as work is becoming more intensive, stressful and less secure, employees are more pressurised, compliant and alienated. This question thus affords students considerable scope in making reasoned and informed responses. Answers could take a general view of what has happened to work and attitudes to work or draw on specific case studies of organisations where attitudes to work may have been modified through the adoption of specific people management practices.

General coverage might draw on concepts such as:

- The psychological contract or expectations of behaviour, relationships and treatment at work. A strong psychological contract provides a sense of identity, offers recognition for employee contribution and conveys a sense of security. A breach of the expectations of the psychological contract can result in a loss of trust and a sense of betrayal. Research (for example, Herriot and Pemberton 1995) suggests that the psychological contract has been damaged through an intensification of work, increased stress and longer hours and has contributed to feelings of employee disempowerment and powerlessness and low levels of trust. Feelings of insecurity and disempowerment fuel a more instrumental short-term and cynical attitude to work and employment, and lower levels of commitment and loyalty.

- The work/life balance, a campaign launched by the DTI in 2000 to promote flexible working arrangements. This initiative reflects wider social attitudes that a combination of external and internal factors (effects of technology, excessive hours worked, stressful nature of work) was damaging for both individuals and organisations.

- The emergence of a more demanding workforce as a result of generational differences to work, career and employment. Taylor (2002) suggests that the attitudes of the so-called Generation Y carry important consequences for organisations seeking to recruit and retain young people. He identifies attitudes such as opposition to intolerance, resistance to tight systems of control and support for better work/life balance as resulting in less organisational loyalty, lower acceptance of managerial prerogative and a greater tendency to challenge and question.

The people management responses to changing attitudes to work and employment will depend on the problems/issues identified and the employment philosophy of the organisation. For example within organisations where people are regarded as a commodity and where the nature of the employment relationship is transactional, responses might include new forms of work and job design; a greater use of automated systems to remove the monotony of certain jobs; recruitment of individuals with lower work aspirations. Within professional and knowledge-based organisations, creativity and innovation will be key to competitive success and will require more open corporate communications channels; the development of a high-trust culture; self-managed teams; decentralised decision-making; flexibility in work design and restructuring the work/life balance; protecting intellectual property rights; nurturing commitment and loyalty of a more demanding workforce through genuine participation and involvement. Such approaches are likely to be accompanied by increased outsourcing of routine corporate activities.

November 2003 Section A

Question 1

Read the following material, extracted from *Knowledge management: a state of the art guide* by Paul Gamble and John Blackwell (London: Kogan Page, 2001), and answer the questions beneath.

Some seven or eight years ago, researchers at a major pharmaceutical company developed the washing powder tablet. The chemists who developed the idea did not think much of it since they hardly regarded it as a technical challenge. They knew how to make washing soaps into nice granular format; they had been doing so for years and understood the chemistry through and through. Combining these products into a tablet was not new chemistry; just a reformulation of stuff that already existed. Done it, Tick that box. Ideally, the chemists should have talked to the marketing people rather than prejudge whether the customers (lay people) would have the same conception of the product as they did.

Shortly afterwards the chemists in Unilever (a major rival) came up with the same idea. However, Unilever was able to connect the research chemists and their tablet with the marketing people who actually made the mind jump needed. They recognised the market potential of a good idea and stole a thumping great share of the market. The first pharmaceutical company is still trying to recover.

(a)   *Compare the experiences described here with the available research into the factors that make 'knowledge management' work and the factors that inhibit its success. Why are people who have valuable knowledge often reluctant to share it with others?*

(b)   *What lessons could be learned in your own organisation from the events described above?*

Section A questions often focus on a particular organisational context. Here it was a pharmaceutical company that had missed a business opportunity by not harnessing the knowledge and capabilities of key employees. The consequences for the company were dramatic and far-reaching. The response to this question should be framed within this context with the obvious focus on knowledge management. Paying attention to context is important and reduces the risk of producing generalised answers. As the case illustrates, the key to effective knowledge management is ensuring that the right type of knowledge is shared. Where activities are complex such as in new product development and knowledge is tacit and dependent on creativity and expertise, the organisational benefits can be significant. However, the process of knowledge sharing is often complicated, contested and contingency constrained.

A good answer would thus have acknowledged the importance of context in knowledge transfer and highlighted the factors contributing to the success of knowledge management as:

- cultural norms that emphasise the importance of sharing knowledge

- a climate of trust, commitment and involvement

- IT systems that capture and codify tacit and explicit knowledge

- team working, networks and communities of practice

- processes of organisational learning which support and assist in knowledge sharing.

Factors inhibiting knowledge transfer could include structural factors, for instance, traditional hierarchies which inhibit collaboration and communication; cultural factors, for example, blame cultures which inhibit challenge, reflection and innovation and managers who fail to exhibit trust and respond to suggestions; psychological factors, for instance, expertise may be guarded as a source of personal power, status and remuneration (further information can be obtained from www.brint.com/km/ ; www. kmbook.com).

Structuring the answer around broad headings and providing illustrative examples reflects a more analytical approach that simply listing factors.

It is important to recognise that this question was in two parts and that both parts carried equal marks and should therefore have received equal amounts of attention. The second part of the question required an analysis of the implications of the case scenario for the candidate's own organisation. Good answers would have provided an outline of the context of the chosen organisation and gone on to critically evaluate the degree to which knowledge sharing was practiced, followed by specific guidance on how the named organisation might be addressing stated goals and aspirations. Answers that merely reproduced corporate rhetoric about aspirations for sharing knowledge would not have scored highly.

Question 2

Read the following material, extracted from 'It takes two to review' by David Butcher (*Management Today*, November 2002) and answer the questions beneath.

For a process that's so well established in the corporate landscape, the performance appraisal is astonishingly unpopular. Employees dread it as an annual calling-to-account, a sinister session where they'll have to defend their record, bat off criticism and make a desperate pitch for a pay rise. Managers, on the other hand, see it as a bureaucratic chore, an hour of ticking boxes and mouthing platitudes that could be better spent on other things. According to the Chartered Institute of Personnel and Development (CIPD), one in eight managers would actually prefer to visit the dentist than carry out a performance appraisal.

The bad news is that reviews are becoming more frequent – bi-annual, quarterly, monthly, and even, in some eager firms, weekly. They have come to be seen as a vital component of a well-tempered company. And like so many once intuitive features of business life, the appraisal has become more and more rigorous: a well oiled machine devised by the folks in HR to calibrate every employee and map out their duties.

(a) *To what extent are the points made here supported or refuted by research into performance appraisal?*

(b) *How far do you recognise any of the arguments advanced by Butcher in the performance review processes used in your own organisation? Give reasons for your views.*

In line with expectations that candidates will be familiar with evidence-based research and practice, section A questions frequently reproduce extracts from specific journals, research reports and other commentaries followed by questions about the extract. This is the format for questions 2 and 3. Question 2 focuses on the drawbacks of performance review and appraisal systems. The question is in two parts and equal time and attention should have been devoted to both parts.

Weightman (2004, p184) summarises the problems associated with performance management and highlights design, structural, procedural and behavioural aspects whereby the effectiveness of performance management can be undermined (examples of research on the topic are also included in response to question B3 of the May 2003 paper).

The second part of the question called for a critical evaluation of the review process within the candidate's organisation. Good answers would demonstrate knowledge, understanding, critical awareness and political sensitivity. The chief examiner's report reproduces the final paragraph of an answer that convincingly demonstrates these competences:

Previously it was a burden, an annual bottleneck of almost meaningless interviews where employees were uncertain of what was happening and why. Now it is an effective two-way communication tool that along with other moves from compliance to commitment has increased morale and 'organisational process advantage'.

(Purcell)

Question 3

Read the following material, extracted from 'Strike the right balance at work', a *Viewpoint* article by Peter Ellwood, CEO of Lloyds TSB (downloaded from FT.com, the *Financial Times* website, on 16 January 2003), and answer the questions beneath.

Voluntary practice is generally preferable to legislation. But legislation can bring change for the better. Take the race relations and sex discrimination acts as examples where perceived bureaucracy has brought real, meaningful benefits to the world of work. In April 2003 new employment rights will come into effect. Among them is the entitlement for working parents with children under the age of 6 to request flexible working arrangements. I believe this legislation presents a great opportunity for many UK organisations to examine how issues such as productivity and staff management affect the bottom line. Independent research shows a compelling business case for pursuing policies that attempt to offer employees better work/life balance. The point is that work/life balance is not a passing fad. Concern over it came about because of pressures on business ... These pressures have not disappeared; in fact all indicators point to their increasing.

(a) *What is the research evidence in favour of a 'compelling business case' for work/life balance policies? How far do you agree with Ellwood when he says that the pressures on business to implement work/life balance policies and practices are likely to increase in the foreseeable future?*

(b) *How well does your own organisation address work/life balance issues? What improvements would be desirable and why?*

This question contains a number of component elements and it is important that each element is addressed fully and convincingly.

First, candidates are asked to identify research evidence supporting the business case for work/life balance (for instance, www.dti.gov.uk/work-lifebalance/; CIPD work/life balance fact sheet). Second, candidates are asked to comment on their support or otherwise for the sentiments expressed in the extract. This required a degree of judgement and evaluation in response to the three specific issues cited namely the business case for work/life balance, the pressures on business that have prompted a concern with work/life balance and the prediction that these are likely to continue. Finally, candidates were asked to evaluate the extent to which their own organisations addressed the work/life balance and to produce justified proposals for improvement. Rather than a generalised statement about the benefits of work/life balance, the question called for the production of specific evidence that addressing work/life balance issues would bring concrete benefits to the individual and organisations. Reference might, for example, been made to Purcell *et al*'s (2003b) study which identified work/life balance as a key policy in triggering discretionary behaviour and above average performance.

November 2003 Section B

Section B of the Managing People exam comprises 10 questions of which seven require answers. Equal marks are awarded to each question and it is important therefore that sufficient time is allocated to each question. Section B questions are more specific and situational and require a focused, direct approach. These are questions calling for professional, business-focused and realistic advice to colleagues and business partners. They often take the form of responses to e-mail messages as is the case here.

> You should assume that you have just arrived at your workstation and switched on your PC. The following 10 e-mail messages appear. You are required to indicate the content of your response to any seven; the manner of your response is not relevant.

Question 1

> *From a friend studying for the CIPD qualification*: Looking at the CIPD's Flexible Learning Support website the other day, I saw a quote from Professor Cary Cooper: 'Organisations have been changing such a lot in the past decade, much of it change for change's sake, and many companies are guilty of poor management of change.' How far does the experience of your own organisation justify what he's saying, so far as people management is concerned? Why do organisations continue to get it wrong?

Candidates were required to comment on the scope and effectiveness of change management. Evidence (for example, CIPD Reorganising for Success project) points to continuous change within organisations but shows that most change initiatives fail to meet their intended objectives of financial return and internal effectiveness. The primary causes of failure are inevitably linked to people management factors. This question afforded candidates considerable scope to write about their experiences of change whether positive or negative. Points made in relation to the reasons for getting it wrong might have included the following:

- lack of a clear strategy
- failure to address implementation issues
- poor project management
- internal conflict
- poor quality leadership
- loss of key staff
- lack of involvement, communication.

Question 2

> *From the IT Manager*: I saw a piece in my journal, *The IT Manager*, reporting a study by Cincom Systems, the business solution producer, which concludes that job satisfaction is now

the main driving force for employee retention, with money third as a motivational factor. How do these findings compare with research evidence from elsewhere?

The *CIPD recruitment and retention report* (2003b) would provide good supporting evidence that drivers of employee retention are rarely to do with money. Key aspects of retention strategies include improved training and development opportunities together with employer branding. This report also highlights the importance of monitoring absence, as this could be an indicator of dissatisfaction. Alternatively, the *CIPD labour turnover report* (2003c) shows that the key reasons for voluntary turnover include career development and progression.

Question 3

> *From the editorial team, Human Resources magazine*: We hope you can help us. We plan to produce an article entitled 'Theory X is Alive and Well, and Living in the UK Economy'. To what extent do you agree, so far as your own organisation is concerned?

To gain marks, candidates should avoid generalisations about theory X management and focus on the extent to which Theory X assumptions about employee attitudes and behaviours and resulting frameworks of management control can be discerned within contemporary organisations. Call centres represent an obvious example where theory X management can be said to be thriving. Call centre work is fragmented, closely monitored, tightly controlled and often induces employees to demonstrate job avoidance behaviours that validate theory X assumptions.

Question 4

> *From the CEO*: Somebody said something intriguing at a conference I attended recently, namely, that 'real leaders are found all over the organisation from the executive suite to the shop floor.' Does the evidence about leadership support this idea? What's more, how could we spot leadership potential on the shop floor?

Ways of spotting leadership on the shop floor include:

- demonstration of discretionary/organisational citizenship behaviour

- initiative in problem solving

- coaching, counselling, mentoring others

- responding to the suggestions of others

- communicating with, involving and guiding others.

The question begins with the assertion that leadership can be present through the organisation and asks for evidence. In essence the question is calling for a conceptualisation of leadership. If, as Weightman (2004, p129) suggests leadership can be defined as the '... ability to get people to do different things from that which they would have done otherwise, and do these things with some degree of commitment and enthusiasm', then the assertion can be supported. However, if leadership is defined as a process of developing and executing the vision and mission of the organisation, planning change and informing policy, then it is likely to be confined to specific senior levels.

Question 5

> *From the Production Manager*: We're planning to introduce a 24-hour, seven-days-a-week shift system shortly. Please advise me about the psychological and physiological problems associated with shift working, and how they can be minimised.

This was a relatively straightforward 'textbook' question with little contextual consideration. The question did not call for a challenge to the validity of 24-hour, seven-day-a-week working or a consideration of alternatives. It required the provision of accurate advice as to the potential problems and practical, realistic and cost-effective solutions.

Good answers would have differentiated between physiological problems (for instance, disruptions to sleep and eating patterns, accumulated fatigue, digestive and neurological problems) and psychological problems (for example, effects on work attitudes, job

satisfaction and job performance, social and domestic disruption).
The contribution of shift working to higher levels of stress can have
both physiological and psychological consequences. Problems could
be minimised through:

- careful selection criteria for shift work (for some individuals
  shift work represents an attractive form of flexibility)

- provision of support services such as health checks, education,
  counselling for shift workers

- monitoring working schedules to ensure the right mix of rest
  breaks and work consistent with the nature of the work and the
  work environment.

Question 6

From the Office Manager: As you know, we only have very
limited space, and it would be easy for me to ask some of my
people to work from home. What does research and experience
tell us about the motivational and people management issues
involved?

The motivation and management issues involved in home working
include consideration of:

- selection criteria of home workers to ensure a fit with personal
  attitudes, values, norms, qualities, needs

- the nature of the work and the fit of technology for the specific
  work role

- the extent to which the business culture supports home working including the willingness and ability of managers to trust
  home workers and accept that day-to-day control is no longer
  practical

- home/work interface, for example, family relations, physical
  space and facilities available, legal and insurance aspects.

Baruch and Nicholson (1997) suggest that each of these factors needs
to be fulfilled simultaneously if home working is to be effective.

Question 7

From the HR Director: I'm concerned about one of the findings in the report, *Working in Britain* (2000), which says that 'Today's world of work is much less satisfying to employees than the one they were experiencing 10 years ago.' Why might this be the case? How far does it apply to employees in our own organisation?

This question calls for a discussion of the general topic as to why the world of work could be less satisfying than 10 years ago together with an evaluation of the applicability and relevance of trends to the candidate's own organisation. The *Working in Britain report* (Economic and Social Research Council, 2000) is part of the ESRC Future of Work Programme and highlights the following trends in the nature of work:

- Most people are employed on a permanent basis and are working longer for the same employer.

- Most people regard their job as part of a career with distinct promotion prospects.

- Loyalty to the organisation is diminishing.

- Greater work intensification – people are working harder and longer and report a dramatic decline in job satisfaction.

- Greater freedom for workers has been combined with a greater degree of control and surveillance by management.

- A growing proportion of the workforce needs advanced, complex IT skills.

Question 8

From the Call Centre Manager: I work hard to encourage teamwork in my department, yet I'm told it sometimes has negative consequences. Can you please outline these possible negative aspects of team working for me, and advise me on how to prevent them?

The question called for both identification of the negative consequences of team working and advice as to how these might be overcome. Equal attention should be given to both aspects. The negative consequences of teamwork might include:

- hostility to new team members

- loyalty to the team at the expense of the organisation

- conflict and competition with other teams

- defensiveness, resistance to change

- group pressure to secure individual conformity to group norms.

These negative consequences might be overcome through:

- careful team selection

- clear specification of team task

- performance measures and priorities

- effective, skilled and sensitive leadership

- use of cross-functional project teams with organisation-wide objectives

- reward/recognition system that acknowledges and reinforces co-operation.

Question 9

From the Finance Director: I'm keen on introducing some motivational ideas which I picked up while working in the USA. My people say they won't work here, but I think that what they really mean is that they don't want these new approaches to work here because they prefer to work in their existing comfort zone. What's your view?

The key requirement of this question was the provision of evidence; whether organisational or research-based, of the success/failure of US-originated ideas and approaches to motivation and the reasons for success/failure. US motivational ideas are based on vision, challenge, recognition, high levels of involvement, participation and collaboration and, as the question suggests, rejection of such approaches may mask resistance to change and unwillingness to move out of existing comfort zones. Candidates should thus have drawn on their own experiences of US-originated ideas and approaches to motivation and discussed factors and reasons making for success or failure. Factors discussed may have included structural, cultural and behavioural elements. Care should have been taken in this question not to resort to unfounded stereotypes and assumptions of US management and management techniques.

Question 10

From the Sales Manager: We've been troubled with labour turnover and poor performance recently, and I've begun to wonder whether we have the right ideas about what sort of people perform well in the sales function. What does the evidence suggest about the personality attributes and motivational patterns that are best suited to effective salespeople?

In answering this question candidates should again have drawn on evidence, either from their own organisation or from their reading, to identify the personality attributes and motivational patterns of effective salespeople. Some consideration should have been given to context since selling highly complex, technical products or processes may call for a different repertoire of attributes than a simple commodity. The personal attributes of effective sales people may have been categorised around empathy; ego-strength (inner drive, self-reliance, motivation); ego-drive (resilience, ability to cope with rejection).

May 2004 Section A

For the May 2004 Managing People paper, examples (from Sections A and B) are provided of actual answers taken from candidate scripts. These answers have been selected because they demonstrate the BACKUP competences.

Question 1

At the CIPD annual conference in 2002, Frank Douglas challenged delegates to question whether they were trying forlornly to create a symphony orchestra in their organisations when what they really needed was a jazz band. In an orchestra there is a central direction and a single composition to be played in accordance with the composer's instructions, whereas a jazz band will typically permit greater improvisation by individual players, so different models of leadership will be found in each.

(a)   *How far is the challenge presented by Frank Douglas supported by the available research into what motivates people in high-performing organisations?*

(b)   *Giving reasons for your views assess whether your own organisation resembles an 'orchestra' or a 'jazz band'. What are the implications so far as people performance and commitment are concerned?*

Answer

(a) Research funded by the CIPD into 12 organisations has shown that high performance organisations have a natural inclination towards Frank Douglas' 'jazz band'. The research was reported in *People Management* and is entitled 'Performance – Unlocking the Black Box'. The research shows that in high-performance organisations it is a combination of human capital advantage, gained through recruitment, development and retention strategies, and organisational process advantage which the essential component. Organisational process advantage is concerned with the added value that can be gained from the systems and processes in the workplace. However, the research suggests it is not the systems and processes that add value but the way in which people work together – I feel that this is a perfect comparison with the 'jazz band'.

The research looked at the differences between the performances of four separate Tesco stores. Questionnaires were given to all staff and the results were analysed. Tesco has a philosophy of top-down management, which it believes is the most successful method of instilling the values in all of its employees, the leadership is strong and by way of empowering people through the promotion of the 'values in action' Tesco, so the research indicates, has a committed workforce. However, the differences in performance between the four stores were remarkable and this correlates with the opinions of staff, as drawn from the attitude surveys. The research concluded that it was the immediate line managers that were having the greatest effect on employee motivation, performance and commitment.

In the light of the research, I disagree with the inference that a 'central direction', a 'single composition' and a 'composer's instructions' do not permit greater improvisation by individual players. 'Unlocking the Black Box' has shown that in high performance organisations, the essential components are strong leadership, highly communicated and believed values, rigid structures, processes and systems but an added ability for line managers to breathe life into these structures and by doing so, gain committed and motivated staff. The stores that did not have this extra component of line management styles did not perform as well. The research also found that Tesco, Nationwide and Selfridges gave their employees a voice, welcomed ideas and innovation and encouraged ability and motivation through providing opportunities for staff to develop themselves and to listen to ideas.

(b) I work for a subsidiary of X called Y. From what I have witnessed of X, they have an 'orchestral' approach to their values, systems and procedures. By introducing a shared services function for HR, finance, procurement and IT as the result of an acquisition, it is attempting to unite its employees into one machine. In doing this, I feel the company is risking losing the existing team working atmosphere that currently exists.

In contrast to X, Y is different, perhaps because it is out of scope of the shared services programme. We have a strong, personable, approachable and inspirational leader who has high values and expectations of his teams. The management team thrive on this and also impart the 'electricity' the MD imparts. It would be unrealistic of me to tell you that all 457 employees are the most committed and high performing, however, I am most confident in my interactions with line managers and staff across functions that there is a huge element of motivation to work and a commitment to the business. Indeed this year has seen remarkable profits of £10m, sickness absence is down to 2.75 per cent, non-productive time has fallen to 8 per cent and we have an excellent accident frequency rate and environmental rate. Comparing this with further years of the business when we were more of an integral part of X, I hope I have made my point. After all X has a turnover rate of 16.8 per cent compared with Y of 4.8 per cent.

Question 2

Writing in *People Management*, Jeffrey Pfeffer has described the 'doing–knowing gap' – the practice of doing without knowing, i.e., taking action based on half-truths and possibly false assumptions rather than clear evidence and hard facts.

According to Pfeffer, 'Management practice should be based on evidence, not beliefs or ideology ... If taken seriously, evidence-based management can change how every manager thinks and acts. It is a way of seeing the world and using business knowledge that can drive every firm to make better decisions, take wiser actions and, as a side benefit, treat people better.'

- *(a)*   *How far do you agree with Pfeffer's claim that 'Management practice should be based on evidence, not beliefs or ideology'?*
- *(b)*   *Using examples from its people-management strategies and practices, assess the extent to which your own organisation exemplifies the 'doing–knowing gap' and indicate what could be done to avoid the consequential problems.*

Answer

(a) Pfeffer has been accredited as being one of the 'excellence' authors and many of his studies are regularly reported. One study he carried out in America related to the links he believed were present between profit, shareholder return and people management practices. His study showed that 7 HR practices made the difference in financial terms when these US based organisations had them in place. They are:

- employment security
- careful recruitment
- team based focus and decentralised organisation
- high pay with an incentive element
- extensive training
- narrow status differentials
- lots of communication.

If we are to believe this study then this should be replicated and results from this evidence would lead to increased financial results. However, his evidence has been disputed by the contingency theorists/researchers who believe that there is a contingency element that is missing and in some cases the belief is that it should be based on bundles of policies, the sum is greater than the parts.

The evidence from the Black Box report and the CIPD commissioned reports of 2003 is that the 'Big Idea' is one of the key differentiators to success for organisations. Would this evidence achieve that? Beliefs and ideology do relate to vision and culture of the organisation and therefore can be seen to have a contingent element. It is also to be recognised that there is so much evidence about that states what works and what doesn't. Not all organisations are the same, so I do believe that while evidence does give you a steer in the right direction, only by looking at beliefs and ideology when it relates to culture and contingency on organisation and leader can you really affect superior management practice.

(b) Within my own organisation there has been a considerable drive to increase the amount of evidence and hard facts that drive, e.g., performance management. We have introduced over the last 12–18 months the service profit and morale measurement system in many areas. This seeks to provide productivity information, service levels and morale measures. As with all these types of measure it:

- Is not always a true reflection of actual activity.
- Morale can change daily.
- Problems with the same questions asked.
- Dealing with service levels in terms of call duration does not always reflect quality of service.

We therefore have to be sure that we are able to interpret results fairly and accurately and not just that we have evidence to judge. In the call centre environment where measures such as call duration, numbers of calls taken per hour are used as performance measures; they can not only cause stress and dissatisfaction but also ultimately lead to a poor service for the customer. The process of call cutting to inflate results has been a real issue for management. Therefore, yes, we do need evidence but it is all too easy for that to slip into half truths if we don't take the time to reflect the whole picture.

We therefore, not only need to interpret statistics but we have to see what makes the real difference for customers and our employees. How can we use the statistics to guide without quashing employees? In some areas the statistics have been altered to look at output rather than pure statistics i.e. number of converted sales or number of satisfied customers through our customer survey. We need to improve and maybe, as some companies have done, we need to challenge the use of these measures altogether and allow ourselves to trust our operators to perform and work well for the organisation.

Question 3

Read the following passage, extracted from an e-mail news-letter published by Management Centre Europe (http://www. mce.be), and answer the questions beneath.

Knowledge, skills and talent are different. Knowledge and skills are transferable from person to person but they tend to be specific to the situation. Talents are transferable from situation to situation but are specific to the person. A manager's job is not to give people talent – rather it is to select the right talent for the role and then to build it into a strength and knowledge. In every role there is range, and it is talent that causes someone to excel in a role. Only talent can account for the range in performance.

(a)   *Giving reasons for your views and drawing on relevant evidence and research where you can, indicate the extent to which you agree with these three propositions:*

(i) knowledge and skills tend to be specific to the situation
(ii) talents are transferable from situation to situation
(iii) 'only talent can account for the range in performance'.
(b) How far are the views expressed here, about knowledge, skills and talent, applied in your own organisation? What changes would you recommend in order to optimise the use of talent?

Answer

(a) (i) To an extent I agree that knowledge and skills are specific to the situation. In particular technical knowledge is. For example, an IT consultant trained in one computer language can only apply that knowledge to situations involving computers in that language. Some skills are also situation specific. For example a machine operator may only know how to operate a specific machine in a specific factory. However, knowledge and skill can also be transferable. As an OD Consultant I can apply my knowledge of teams to any team I work with regardless of what they do. The same is true of skills, particularly people management skills such as influencing and presenting.

The competency movement has added value by stipulating the things people should be able to understand or do in order to perform in a given role. This sets out many of the skills and knowledge required. To conclude, I think that technical or functional knowledge and skills are more specific to the situation however, people management skills are less specific.

(ii) There is a current trend to 'recruit for attitude and develop skills'. In a similar way this statement seems to advocate a similar approach to talent. This partly depends on the definition of talent. Is it an innate ability? If so is it related to current performance or potential? Assuming that talent is a propensity towards competence in a given task, I think that it is transferable. However, talent is very difficult to define and distinguish from knowledge, skills and abilities.

(iii) I think that this statement is not plausible. There are many other factors that influence performance including:

- clarity of objectives
- overlap of business and personal objectives
- correct training and development

- personal motivation, drawing on Herzberg's motivators
- coaching and support from line manager
- personal ambition and drive for success.

(b) This debate is highly relevant to my organisation, ABC financial services. There are several Initiatives aimed at addressing this. Firstly, an emphasis on a new performance management process and development planning. This is to ensure that all colleagues are clear on what's expected of them and have a plan in place to address any gaps that may be knowledge, skills or behaviours. Secondly, the HR department is introducing a development framework to help colleagues identify their learning needs and to suggest development options that are specific to the profession. Finally, our talent management team are helping managers to identify their top and bottom 10 per cent performers and to ensure that they have a plan in place to support them.

In addition, I would recommend a job analysis of roles, following a recent restructure. This is because many roles have changed significantly and this would clarify expectations. I would recommend using competences to identify skills and knowledge and competencies to form the personal specification that would outline the personal attributes and behaviours of the ideal candidate. The process would need to involve line managers. I think that line managers would benefit from being clearer about the skill and knowledge requirement of their staff. In addition staff would have a firm foundation for performance management, personal development and career progression. Currently we only use poorly defined 'role profiles' that are generic role descriptions. In my company talent is defined as current performance plus potential. The 'talent' that is increasingly sought after is leadership skills as defined as Kotter as setting visions and direction, inspiring and motivating and communicating the visions.

As described in February's *People Management* article, this 'distributive leadership' model is required in a 'networked' organisation such as mine. This requires a focus on the business context, the learner's needs and needs of the business. Our flagship programme takes an action learning approach to developing these skills by creating a collaborative, business focused approach that is owned by participants. This also includes our executive team in setting the business challenges to be addressed by the participants.

May 2004 Section B

You should assume that you have just entered your office at the start of the working day and switched on your PC. The following e-mail messages appear on the screen. You are required only to indicate the content of your response for your chosen seven questions; the method you would use in order to convey your reply is not relevant.

Question 1

From your mentor: You may believe that leadership skills can be developed, but Manfred Kets de Vries argues that many real-life leaders have had a determined mother and a remote or absent father, and that two-thirds of British prime ministers have lost a parent early in life. Surely this suggests that leadership is innate, a product of early life experiences, rather than anything else?

Answer

A great deal has been written on the topic of leadership and one such belief is that leaders are born leaders. There is a whole debate about the difference between managers and leaders and that managers are not necessarily leaders and vice versa. The argument being put forward in the question is that leaders are born leaders, that their leadership ability is the product of their early life experiences. Evidence from writers such as Watson and Kotter believe the leadership involves the soft people skills that some, but not all, people possess. A recent phenomenon in leadership theory is that of Emotional Intelligence and I believe that this theory backs up the point made in the question that leadership is innate. Daniel Goleman coined the concept of Emotional Intelligence and he believes that someone with a low emotional intelligence do not have the skills required to be a great leader. For example, someone could be very highly intelligent and know a lot about the world but if you put them in a room with a group of people and they cannot interact with people or lead the group then they are said to have a low emotional intelligence and would not make an effective leader. This is all about personality and how you can make your emotions work for you in work situations, it is about the 'intelligent use of emotions' (Shukla). If someone has a high emotional intelligence then they will be very good leaders, good at interacting with people, developing people and generally using their emotions to their advantage. Using the concept of emotional intelligence I would tend to agree that leadership is innate. You cannot learn how to interact properly with people, you should be able to do it naturally and this will be the product of early life experiences.

Question 2

From the Marketing Director: When I look around me at truly great organisations, they have one thing in common: their people know and live by their corporate values. I know we have some core values, but how can we make sure that these values are embedded in people's behaviour throughout the organisation?

Answer

Core values and how they can be embedded in the organisation
- Clear vision from the top and message of what the core values are.
- Reflect these values in the people that are recruited.
- Reinforce the values in the way managers from the CEO down behave – walk the talk, actions speak louder than words.
- Reinforce the values in the induction and training of employees.
- Reward and recognise these values in the performance management system and in the way we celebrate success.

- The way we treat customers internally and externally need to reflect the values.
- All marketing, corporate words and speak must reflect these values.
- External representations.
- How we react to our social responsibility to the wider community must reflect these values.
- Communication and lots of it so that the values are known, understood, reflected in behaviour and actions.

Question 3

From the Business Development Manager: I know that team working is vital to our success, but what does the research tell us about ways in which we can create an authentic team spirit when colleagues are working across different continents and time zones?

Answer

There is a need when dealing with people across different locations, undertaking remote working to find other ways of communicating, sharing and participating than in a straightforward face to face basis. Communication is the key – technology can play a big part in the breaking down of physical barriers e.g. e-mail, teleconference and videoconference. There will be a need to meet face to face as well as there is nothing to replace that 'getting to know' someone as a visual, verbal and physical presence. Suggest meeting up at least twice a year or more if practicable and affordable. The team needs a clear vision, objectives set, targets agreed, follow ups and feedback undertaken across the team, success celebrated, not always business discussed, review and feedback are critical to ensure that staff do feel part of the team. One way to supplement the team spirit is to encourage team reward through incentives either monetary or via verbal recognition which can be as powerful. Other ways could be joint collaboration on projects, the need to work closely on specific pieces of work. Involvement, clear roles and responsibilities, reward and recognition are the key.

Question 4

From a fellow CIPD student: Maslow's hierarchy of needs dates
from 1943, and Herzberg's Motivation-Hygiene theory from
1959. Has anything new been said since about the motivation of
people at work, or have Maslow and Herzberg said it all?

Answer

Maslow's hierarchy of needs theory and Herzberg's motivational theory has long been the cornerstone of the motivation
issue. They are still valid. Maslow's idea that as humans we
all have certain needs that must be satisfied in order to
achieve and survive is not a theory specific to work but it is
relevant. People need to satisfy their basic needs before they
can set about satisfying their need for belonging, self achievement etc. The nature of human beings has not changed in this
respect. Herzberg's motivational theory has more relevance
to the workplace. We all have intrinsic and extrinsic needs
which employment must meet to satisfy us. Employees may
have a good job, clear authority, good pay but if they are not
combined with comfortable surroundings and facilities the
employee is not fully satisfied. These two theories are very
relevant but as you say are a little old. There are many examples of other motivational theories. Vroom's expectancy
theory looks at what our expectations are and how much we
want them. Vroom argues that if we want something enough
we work harder to achieve it. Adams equity theory suggests
that we are all motivated by the need for equity (of course
equity can mean different things to different people). Equity
in responsibility and pay. This does not mean to say that we
are motivated by excess, indeed most people are happy to
receive what they consider to be 'fair'. Perhaps you will have
heard of the results of Watson Wyatt employees who believe
they are too well paid! Their motivation is not financial.
Latham and Locke advocate that the great motivators are
goals and feedback. I think we can agree with this. Having
objectives gives us a reason and recognition and spurs us
on to greater things. Therefore, there are many theories on

motivation at work to consider. I believe that they can all have some relevance today.

Question 5

From a professional colleague whom you met at a CIPD branch event: I've just started work for an advertising agency which depends on a constant flow of innovative and sometimes revolutionary thinking. The Directors are worried that we're losing our edge; what does the available research tell us about the things we need to do in order to ensure that our creativity remains high?

Answer

How to keep creativity high?
- Need to create an environment conducive to learning. One company introduced 'incubators' to help generate ideas. These were separate units to the everyday work, where the sole purpose was to come up with new ideas and implement these.
- Need a leadership style that will encourage this. On Tannebaum and Schmidt's continuum, leaders need to give employees freedom to make decisions without management control.
- Empowerment – need to empower staff with enough authority and resources to do their job.
- Offer incentives to staff for new ideas. At (named company) we have a 'New Ideas Programme' where staff receive prizes ranging up to a TV for ideas that add value to the business.
- Need to recruit creative people. Use competency interviews and assessments at the recruitment stage.
- Offer training course to encourage it. For example at (named company) they provide 'business process improvement' training to encourage people to look for more efficient ways of doing things.

All of the above have a cost attached to them, but creativity brings success, innovations before competitors. HR would be involved in arranging most.

Question 6

From the Contact Centre Manager: The attrition rate among our 1,000 staff has just risen to more than 80 per cent. Exit interviews indicate that the principal cause is poor job design, but nobody seems to know what to do about it. Can you help us by outlining a few of the key research findings about 'good' job design and what these findings could mean for us?

Answer

It is starting to become accepted that people need to be able to bring a degree of creativity and discretion to their work in order for them to attach meaning to what they are doing and not be diminished by the routine of uninspiring jobs. It is important therefore to realise that the design of each job will hold different levels of inspiration and motivation for different individuals. One good piece of research has been done by Hackman who points to the idea of investing jobs with meaning by increasing the following emphasis:

- Task significance – so people feel their work has point beyond the duties involved with completing it.
- Variety of skills – making sure the job draws on different attributes of the workers to keep them challenged.
- Autonomy – providing the workers with responsibility so they move towards pride and ownership in what they are doing.
- Task identity – to engender in people the need to complete tasks and projects

Furthermore, it is felt that using these principles, you can map the design of the job on to a framework that enlarges the work, enriches it and even interchanges it with other jobs so that people are more challenged by their work and feel more empowered to make a difference in what they do. A good example I came across in our call centre (named company) was allowing the operatives to 'account manage' areas of branches that they were taking reservations for so they could spend an hour each day liaising with those branches to check on their CSI and how specific customers were handled after the reservation was taken.

Finally and crucially, it is important to not isolate the workers at the call centre from the business they are supporting and include them in communications related to the business performance and changes so they can feel an impact of their contribution. In any role, creating this inclusiveness and involvement in the work has the potential to galvanise the workforce. Research in all areas of discussion on retention figures, shows the involvement of workers in the design of their jobs and their rewards as a worthwhile consideration in how to make work more attractive, rewarding and central.

Question 7

From a researcher at London Business School: We're seeking views about our hypothesis that one of the components of a 'healthy' organisation is that people relationships are adult/adult. Why are some organisations characterised by other kinds of relationships, and what can be done about it?

Unfortunately there were no responses to this question that could be used as examples.

Question 8

From a staff writer at Human Resources magazine: We're planning a feature about the 'work ethic.' Many observers consider that the 'work ethic' has declined: on the basis of the evidence available, how far do you agree?

Answer

It is unclear that work ethic has declined. The CIPD has suggested that how hard people work (work intensification) and the hours people work has made aggregate increases. This suggests no diminishing universal work ethic. However, the form of the psychological contract between employee and employer may have changed and whilst people will work intensively and commit to long hours their long-term loyalty has eroded. People will deliver for the organisation, and CIPD (quick facts) have suggested that employees are delivering work-effort; they just require a different set of rewards and motivations from their employers. One concluding point to make would be from a 2001 Gallup poll that made the distinction between only 20 per cent of employees being engaged with their work and 80 per cent being either non or disengaged. It would be easy to mistake this disaffection for work as poor work ethic when in fact research suggests three-quarters of managers feel they could not work any harder.

This all serves to leave me ambivalent on the idea of a declining work ethic and makes me feel more that people do and want to work hard but just need to be inspired to do so in their working environments.

Question 9

From the Graduate Recruitment Manager: I've just seen some research which suggests that over 60 per cent of new graduates would prefer to work for a smaller company – and we are a large one. Why do they hold such attitudes, and what can we do about the situation so far as our organisation is concerned?

Answer

The predominant feature of the workforce today is that they want to feel valued and they want their job to be satisfying not just for themselves but also for the company as a whole. I would perhaps suggest that graduates coming in to the workplace believe that the attitudes and culture of smaller organisations will lend themselves more easily and fully to this idea than multinational or large organisations which can be seen as impersonal and profit driven. In reality, this is not the case as companies both small and large are making efforts to make themselves 'people friendly' and employers of choice.

For ourselves, I would suggest that we establish a reputation for looking after our employees, advertise ourselves as doing so and most importantly do so when we get the graduates in.

Ideas to look at:

* Invest in our people – put together a personal training and development programme and encourage our staff to develop their knowledge and skills not only to benefit us but also to give them a sense of achievement and employability (Kanter).
* Provide flexible working patterns so that staff have the opportunity to combine work and life outside. Such initiatives have proved to increase productivity and motivation. Staff are not torn between the two aspects of their life and can devote their time to work better. With graduates the idea of offering sabbaticals or training opportunities will be attractive.
* Offer 'well-being' initiatives. Encourage health and exercise. Take an interest in the well-being of staff and make them feel valued.
* Performance management initiatives to reward and feedback recognition and achievement. Employees are looking for employers that value them.
* Pay market rate for job which has clear and defined role.

Question 10

From the Chief Executive: I'm an accountant by training, and my professional colleagues are always very sceptical about the bottom-line benefits resulting from effective people-management practices. Please summarise one piece of research that shows a clear causal link between such practices and organisational performance, so that in future I have some ammunition with which to refute their arguments.

Answer

David Guest produced some research on the relation between people management and organisational performance for the CIPD. This is just one of a number of research studies which indicates that there is a correlation. Guest advocated that companies that invest in a robust people management scheme have seen real and tangible benefits in corporate performance. These benefits include:

- happier, more satisfied workforce
- better customer care
- higher productivity
- lower costs of absenteeism.

The research concluded that there are four key points in effective people management:

- Organisations need to invest in their staff.
- Organisations need to acquire the skills necessary to achieve corporate goals.
- Expected behaviours need to be defined to enable everyone to work together.
- Employers need to gain the commitment of their employees.

From the research available, it is clear that by taking an interest in the individual and developing them in the best interests of the business, organisational performance can benefit. Human capital, not financial, is the future driving force of an organisation. It is for every company to acknowledge and use this to its competitive advantage.

SECTION 4

CONCLUSION

5 CONCLUSION

There has been a lot to read in this book, and although there are clear and consistent messages here, you could be forgiven for feeling confused. So what are the key messages you should take away? In essence, there are 10 of them.

1. You must approach your studies, your performance as a professional and your examination answers, as a Thinking Performer. This means that whatever you are told (by your tutors, by your seniors at work and implicitly by the procedures that underpin your everyday activities) you must evaluate – to determine whether it makes sense, whether it achieves worthwhile objectives, whether it stacks up against evidence from elsewhere, whether it adds value. And if you have doubts, you must articulate them, not least in the examination, where the presence of critical, evaluative and analytical faculties is absolutely essential.

2. You must actively demonstrate your allegiance to the five 'BACKUP' performance criteria: business orientation, application capability, knowledge of the subject matter, understanding in depth and persuasion/presentation skills. Remember that the examiner cannot know that you possess these capabilities unless you demonstrate them to him or her. If your script suggests that you cannot produce sensible proposals to solve a problem or take advantage of an opportunity, the examiner is entitled to conclude that you are not equipped with application capability attributes, and will mark your material accordingly. Similarly, if you appear uninformed about significant issues, themes and topics, the examiner will conclude that you are inadequately prepared for the examination, and will mark your material accordingly. It is important to note, too, that the five 'BACKUP' criteria are very relevant to your professional performance at work: their significance, in other words, is not confined merely to CIPD examinations.

3. You should remember that the display of positive, businesslike attitudes is ultimately as important as the possession of large

quantities of factual knowledge. When the examiner is confronted by scripts that reflect a borderline position between pass and fail, the attitudes and values reflected in the answers may make an essential difference to the final outcome. These attitudes should exemplify the '2 + 10 + 5 + M' model that has been described in detail earlier in the book.

4. In preparing for the examination you should aim to achieve a mark of at least 60 per cent, and should definitely not content yourself with a 'satisficing' strategy of seeking a bare pass. Many individuals have failed in the past because they took unnecessary risks with their preparation, and perhaps found that the more discursive questions commonly found in Section A caused them some problems and helped produce final marks of fewer than 50 per cent. This has meant that they have had to take the examination again – which means another round of study, revision, examination practice and nervous anxiety – and you would not want that to happen to you, would you?

5   There is no fundamental reason why you should be frightened of taking this (or any other examination) if you have prepared yourself thoroughly. People are frightened of examinations because (a) they know in their hearts that they are vulnerable because they have only a sketchy command of the subject matter, or (b) they have not taken examinations before, or have done so very infrequently. Neither of these causes is inevitable. If you have prepared yourself conscientiously, and if you have practised your examination techniques, then you have nothing to fear. What that means, too, is that your performance will improve even more, because fear gets in the way of concentration.

6. You must take the trouble to learn about the practice of People Management in organisations other than your own, and in business sectors other than the one in which you are currently employed. The purpose of the CIPD qualification is not merely, not even principally, to prepare you for the competent discharge of your duties in your existing role, but to prepare you for any future role in any type of organisation. In other words, professional versatility is a core part of the goal for the CIPD – as it

should be for you, too, since nobody can guarantee that their job will last forever, or that their organisation will survive forever.

7. When practising with past examination questions, always leave your work for 24 hours before evaluating it, and always seek to produce answers that combine all the essential ingredients of impressive responses. Leaving your work for 24 hours will enable you to attain that necessary attitude of critical detachment that is a prelude to effective assessment; and the ingredients of impressive responses will generally comprise a measure of each of the following: some factual knowledge relevant to the question's subject-matter; some intelligent, balanced discussion; one or two references to third-party sources of research, evidence or reinforcing literature; a 'live' organisational example; and some 'solutions' to whatever problem the question has posed. Of course, not every answer should possess all these ingredients, but many of them should – and on balance your script as a whole should have a mix of these factors.

8. When generating recommendations or proposals for action, always present your ideas confidently and assertively. Never use words like 'hopefully', but seek to convey the thought that you have the courage of your convictions. One of the principal techniques of persuasion is assertiveness: if you are seeking to convince others of the legitimacy of your views, you will not do it if your views are articulated in a half-hearted, indecisive fashion.

9. Collect material widely, keep your reading up-to-date and ask questions. You should regularly read each issue of *People Management* and any other periodicals, journals, newspapers and other publications you can lay your hands on; you should collect cuttings and download relevant material from the Internet; you should participate in the on-line discussion groups that form such a lively part of the CIPD's website; you should keep asking questions and in particular the two key questions, 'Why do we ...?' and 'Why don't we ...?' True, being constantly inquisitive can make you a bit of a nuisance to your colleagues, but it will undoubtedly help you learn.

10. Focus your thinking on those people-management and people-leadership policies and practices that help to unleash the potential

presently lying dormant in many a human machine at work. Earlier in this book we have outlined the difference between the provision of those 'infrastructure' ingredients that necessarily underpin the work environment, and the 'differentiators' that encourage 'discretionary' behaviour and 'organisational citizenship' action. Organisations need both; some provide neither; some evidently think that the 'infrastructure' of legal and ethical compliance is the only dimension that matters; a few, with penetrating insight, pay attention to the whole picture. If you do the same, you cannot go wrong.

BIBLIOGRAPHY AND USEFUL WEBSITES

ADAIR, J. (1982) *Action-centred leadership*. Aldershot: Gower.

ADAIR, J. (1998) *Leadership skills.* London: CIPD.

ALIMO-METCALFE, B. and ALBAN-METCALFE, J. (2003) Under the influence. *People Management*. 6 March. 32–35.

ARMISTEAD, C., KIELY, J., HOLE, L. and PRESCOTT, J. (2002). An exploration of managerial issues in call centres. *Managing Service Quality*. Vol. 12, No. 4. 246–56.

BARUCH, Y. and NICHOLSON, M. (1997) Home sweet work. *Journal of General Management*, Vol. 23, No. 2. 15–30.

BATT, R. and MOYNIHAN, L. (2002) The viability of alternative call centre production models. *Human Resource Management Journal*. Vol.12, No. 4. 14–34.

BENNIS, W. (2000) *Managing the dream: reflections on leadership and change*. Wokingham: Addison-Wesley.

BENNIS, W. and BIERDERMAN, P. (1997). *Organising genius: the secrets of creative collaboration*. Wokingham: Addison-Wesley.

BOXALL, P. and PURCELL, J. (2003) *Strategy and human resource management.* Basingstoke: Palgrave Macmillan.

BUCKINGHAM, M. (2001) What a waste. *People Management*. 11 October.

CARRINGTON, L. (2002) At the cutting edge. *People Management*. 16 May. 31.

CIPD (2001) *Raising UK productivity: why people management matters.* London: CIPD.

CIPD (2002a) *Employee absence 2002: survey of management policy and practice*. London: CIPD.

CIPD (2002b) *Evaluating human capital: research summary*. London: CIPD. Online version also available at: www.cipd.co.uk.

CIPD (2003a) *Overview of CIPD surveys, 2002/03: HR trends and prospects.* London: CIPD.

CIPD (2003b) *CIPD recruitment and retention report*. London: CIPD.

CIPD (2003c) *CIPD labour turnover report*. London: CIPD.

CIPD (2003d) *Delivering public services, engaging and energising people:*

the change agenda. Online version also available at: www.cipd.co.uk/changeagendas.

CIPD/REWARD GROUP (1999) Benefiting from a balanced life? *CIPD Survey Report* 10. October. London: CIPD.

COYLE-SHAPIRO, J. and KESSLER, I. (2000) Consequences of the psychological contract for the employment relationship. *Journal of Management Studies*. Vol. 37, No.7. 903–30.

ECONOMIC AND SOCIAL RESEARCH COUNCIL (ESRC) (2000) *Working in Britain.* London: ESRC.

EISENHARDT, K. M. and SULL, D. (2001) Strategy as simple rules. *Harvard Business Review*, January–February.

EUROPEAN CENTRE FOR CUSTOMER STRATEGIES (ECCS) (2003) *Sharing the pleasure, sharing the pain*. London: ECCS.

GILLEN, T. (2002) *Leadership skills for boosting performance.* London: CIPD.

GRINT, K. (1993) What's wrong with performance appraisals? A critique and a suggestion. *Human Resource Management*. Vol. 3, No. 3. 61–77.

GUEST, D. (2001) *Public and private sector perspectives on the psychological contract*. London: CIPD.

GUEST, D., MICHIE, J., SHEEHAN, M., CONWAY, N. and METOCHI, M. (2000) *Effective people management: initial findings of the future of work study*. London. CIPD.

HAMMER, M. and CHAMPY, J. (1993) *Re-engineering the corporation: a manifesto for business revolution*, London: Nicholas Brealey.

HERRIOT, P. and PEMBERTON, C. (1995) *New deals*. Chichester: Wiley.

HIGGS, M. and ALLEN, R. (2003) Good call. *People Management*. January.

HOLBECHE, L. (1999) *Aligning human resources and business strategy*. Oxford: Butterworth Heinemann.

HOLLYFORDE, S. and WHIDDETT, S. (2002) *The motivation handbook.* London: CIPD.

HOLMAN, D. (2002). Employee well-being in call centres. *Human Resource Management Journal*. Vol.12, No. 4. 35–50.

HRM International Digest (2000). Vol. 8, No. 5. 4–5.

HUSELID, M. (1995). The impact of human resource management practices on turnover, productivity and corporate financial performance. *Academy of Management Journal*. Vol. 31, No. 3. 625–72.

HUTCHINSON, S. and PURCELL, J. (2003) *Bringing policies to life: the vital role of front line managers in people management*. London: CIPD.

INSTITUTE FOR EMPLOYMENT STUDIES (1999) *Family friendly employment: the business case*. DfEE Research Report 136.

INSTITUTE of DEVELOPMENT STUDIES (IDS) (2000) *Work/life balance*. Study no 698. November.

IDS (2002) Report no. 864. September.

INSTITUTE OF PERSONNEL DEVELOPMENT (IPD) (1994) *People make the difference*. London: IPD.

KAPLAN, R. and NORTON, D. (1996) *The balanced scorecard: translating strategy into action.* Boston, Mass.: Harvard Business School Press.

KAPLAN, R. and NORTON, D. (2001) Marked impact. *People Management*. 25 October.

LONGENECKER, C. (1989) Truth or consequences: politics and performance appraisals. *Business Horizons*. November/December. 76–82.

MOBLEY, W. (1997) Intermediate linkages in the relationship between job satisfaction and employee turnover. *Journal of Applied Psychology*. Vol. 62, No. 2. 237–40.

PETERS, T. and WATERMAN, R. (1982) *In search of excellence: lessons from America's best-run companies*. New York: Harper and Row.

PFEFFER, J. (1998) *The human equation: building profits by putting people first*. Boston, Mass.: Harvard Business School Press.

PORTER, M. (2000) *Can Japan compete?* Basingstoke: Macmillan.

PURCELL, J., KINNIE, N. and HUTCHINSON, S. (2003a) Open minded. *People Management*. 15 May.

PURCELL, J., KINNIE, N., HUTCHINSON, S., RAYTON, B. and SWART, J. (2003b) *Understanding the people performance link: unlocking the black box*. London: CIPD.

REDMAN, T. (2001) Performance appraisal. In REDMAN, T. and WILKINSON, A. (eds). *Contemporary human resource management* pp 57–97. Harlow: FT Prentice Hall.

RICHER, J. (2001) *The Richer way*. London: Richer Publishing.

ROWE, T. (1986) Eight ways to ruin a performance review. *Personnel Journal*. January.

SEMLER, R. (1993) *Maverick: the world's most unusual workplace*. London: Arrow.

SEMLER, R. (2004) *The seven-day weekend: a better way to work in the 21st century*. London: Century.

TAYLOR, R. (2000) *Britain's world of work: myths and realities*. ESRC. Online version also available at: www.esrc.ac.uk.

TAYLOR, S. (2002) *People resourcing*. 2nd edn. London: CIPD.

WEIGHTMAN, J. (2004) *Managing people*. London: CIPD.

WHITE, M. (2000) *Working in Britain in the year 2000*. London: Policy Studies Institute.

WILKINSON, A. (2001) Empowerment. In REDMAN, T. and WILKINSON, A. (eds) *Contemporary human resource management* pp 57–97. Harlow: FT Prentice Hall.

Websites

www.brint.com/km/
www.dti.gov.uk/work-lifebalance/
www.familyfriendly.com
www.kmbook.com
www.pm.gov.uk/
www.worklifebalance.com

INDEX

NOTES